# SMALL GROUP STRATEGIES
## IDEAS & ACTIVITIES FOR DEVELOPING
### SPIRITUAL GROWTH IN YOUR STUDENTS

## LAURIE POLICH & CHARLEY SCANDLYN

ZONDERVAN™

GRAND RAPIDS, MICHIGAN 49530 USA

www.youthspecialties.com

*Small Group Strategies*
Copyright © 2005 by Youth Specialties

Youth Specialties Products, 300 South Pierce Street, El Cajon, CA 92020, are published by
Zondervan, 5300 Patterson Avenue Southeast, Grand Rapids, MI 49530.

**Library of Congress Cataloging-in-Publication Data**

Polich, Laurie.
  Small group strategies : ideas and activities for developing spiritual
growth in your students / by Laurie Polich and Charley Scandlyn.
      p. cm.
  Includes bibliographical references and index.
  ISBN 0-310-25801-4
  1.  Church work with students. 2.  Church group work with youth. 3.
Small groups--Religious aspects--Christianity.  I. Title: Small group
ideas and activities. II. Scandlyn, Charley. III. Title.
  BV4447.P567 2005
  259'.23--dc22

                                                                    2004017087

Unless otherwise indicated, all Scripture quotations are taken from the Holy Bible: New
International Version (North American Edition), copyright © 1973, 1978, 1984 by International
Bible Society. Used by permission of Zondervan Publishing House.

All rights reserved. No part of this publication may be reproduced, stored in a retrieval system,
or transmitted in any form or by any means—electronic, mechanical, photocopy, recording, or
any other—(except for brief quotations in printed reviews) without the prior permission of the
publisher.

Web site addresses listed in this book were current at the time of publication. Please contact
Youth Specialties via e-mail (YS@YouthSpecialties.com) to report URLs that are no longer
operational and replacement URLs if available.

*Editorial direction by Dave Urbanski*
*Art direction by Jay Howver*
*Edited by Laura Gross*
*Proofreading by Anita Palmer*
*Cover design by Burnkit*
*Interior design by Mark Novelli*

*Printed in the United States*

05 06 07 08 09 / DC / 10 9 8 7 6 5 4 3

# TABLE OF CONTENTS

# CHAPTER ONE
# A FEW IMPORTANT WORDS ABOUT SMALL GROUPS

Small groups are not the end of ministry; they are the beginning. Many youth workers believe that if they can get kids into small groups, their job is done. But the real job has just begun. Ministry is about life change, and for this to happen, there needs to be an intentional approach to HOW small groups will nurture and shape students' lives.

Often in youth ministry, success is measured by attendance. But having good attendance isn't what makes your small group ministry successful. It's what happens to your students once they get there. If we don't take the time to answer key questions like, Why are we using this ministry strategy? or What are we hoping to accomplish? we can find ourselves with frustrated leaders, directionless students, and very little life-change. In one small group, after weeks of meeting together, a student asked his leader, "Why are we here anyway?" A question like that—though typical of adolescence—is a sign that something may need to change.

Small groups can be exciting, challenging, and spiritually transforming. But again, they are the starting point of ministry—not the end. Each group needs to have an intentional goal and vision that is embraced by every member.

Before we dig into what that all means, here are three foundational principles every small group leader should understand:

**1. SMALL GROUP MEETINGS ARE VALUE-DRIVEN, NOT CURRICULUM-DRIVEN.** The significance of getting kids to connect is always greater than the goal of finishing a lesson. Therefore, a successful small-group experience is defined by whether or not kids participated in a meaningful discussion, not whether or not the lesson was completed.

How many times have you heard from a small group leader who came equipped with a lesson plan and was ready to fire away—

only to leave discouraged because her students didn't "get into" the meeting? (This is especially frustrating when that leader is you.) All it takes is a long sigh, a distracting comment, or the notorious "nap jerk" to realize you just aren't reaching your audience. And therein lies the problem: Your students have become *an audience.*

Sometimes a leader is unintentionally more committed to the lesson plan than the spiritual growth of the students. This happens when spiritual growth is understood as the *transmission* of information rather than the *understanding* of biblical truth. This basic difference can make a group curriculum-driven rather than values driven.

As a small group leader, it's important to evaluate your group on the basis of your values. This takes some honest thought about what is happening—and what you *want* to happen—in your small group. That's what this book is about.

Your values, whether stated or unstated, will drive your small group ministry. If you don't take the time to explore those values, your small group may reflect values you don't really have. This book will help you develop clearly stated values that make small groups worth leading—and give you ideas and activities for how to experience those values in your group.

**2. SMALL GROUP RELATIONSHIPS ARE MORE IMPORTANT THAN SMALL GROUP ATTENDANCE.** The core of small group ministry is relationships, not attendance. In his book, *God at the Mall*, Pete Ward says, "Relationships are the fuel on which youth work travels. To be engaged in building relationships with young people is an intentional activity."

Leanne loved the other girls in her small group and loved sharing life with them, but when her life fell apart, she pulled back. Leanne didn't want to talk about the mess at home, so she withdrew. Leanne's leader would see her every couple of months at church, but when she asked her to stick around for small group, Leanne always found an excuse to duck out. Two years passed before Leanne was finally willing to come on a trip with her small group. It was then that she recommitted her life to Christ. Her telling comment was, "I can't believe you let me come back. You always let me come back."

## "GOOD LEADERS ARE ALWAYS ON THE LOOKOUT FOR WAYS TO MAKE CONNECTIONS WITH KIDS OUTSIDE THE MEETING"

Small group attendance doesn't guarantee a good relationship between leader and student anymore than a lack of attendance guarantees a lack of relationship. A student can meet with his small group religiously but fail to bring himself to the table. In contrast, a student may have poor attendance, but have a vital connection with the group. Good small group leaders develop relationships with students not only by leading them during the meeting, but also by pursuing them outside of the meeting. Remember Jesus' strategy with his sheep. When 99 showed up, he went looking for the one who didn't.

Jesus lived out this strategy with his disciples in a more profound way. Mark 3:14 says, "He appointed 12—designating them apostles—*that they might be with him*" (emphasis ours). Being with Jesus was the first and most important goal for this renegade small group. The unbelievable invitation of Jesus is that he calls us to a ministry of inviting kids to be with us—so that they can be with him!

**3. SMALL GROUP MINISTRY GOES BEYOND THE SMALL GROUP MEETING.**
Our impact on the lives of kids is not limited to the 70 minutes we have their attention. (Let's make that *seven* minutes for those who work with junior high.) Good leaders are always on the lookout for ways to make connections with kids outside the meeting. If there is a spiritual understanding within the meeting, look for how it can be experienced in the real world of the students. If there is a spiritual or relational deadlock, look for avenues outside the gathering to overcome these obstacles.

> ## "THE MISSION OF A SMALL GROUP LEADER IS TO DEVELOP MEANINGFUL RELATIONSHIPS WITH STUDENTS AND TO HELP SHAPE THEM INTO THE PEOPLE GOD DESIGNED THEM TO BE."

Small group leaders should look for ways to foster spiritual discovery with their students beyond "once-a-week." This requires taking the ministry beyond the four walls of the meeting and placing it in the field where kids live, eat, play, and breathe the stresses of everyday life. This isn't to say that the safety and intimacy of the meeting is not important. Transforming leaders simply look for ways to springboard faith connections into the real world. Conversations with kids during an afternoon of cookie baking can make a bigger impact on them than three weeks of carefully planned curriculum. It's all about having the willingness to move beyond the usual confines into everyday life.

## YOUR MISSION
The mission of a small group leader is to develop meaningful relationships with students and to help shape them into the people God designed them to be. Small group meetings, and the activities and ideas that go along with

them, are not the mission. They are the vehicles we use to accomplish the mission—namely, spiritual transformation in the lives of our kids.

In the following chapters, you will find strategic change to approaches to small group ministry that will help you accomplish this mission. You will learn how to run a small group meeting in such a way so that your students will be ministered to personally and effectively. You will learn not only how to nurture your students' spiritual development by evaluating where they are, but also how to encourage them toward the next step. Finally, you will be equipped with meaningful ideas and activities that are specifically designed to help students live out their faith at every level of spiritual growth.

The goal is clear—your students will discover who Jesus is and embrace the relationship he has for them. While you can't control their spiritual journeys, you can provide a nurturing context for growth to take place. This book will help you do just that.

# CHAPTER TWO
# SMALL GROUP
# MEETINGS

When leading a small group meeting, effective leaders make sure the content serves the mission—not the other way around. We don't do small groups so we can use the latest six-week study guide. Instead, we examine, mold, and shape each study to meet the mission we have for our small group. In later chapters we will talk about our ministry outside the small group meeting. In this chapter, we want to look at the meeting itself.

## PRINCIPLES AND GOALS

We believe there are five goals for a small group meeting that will help you clarify what material to choose and how to use it with your group. Before we look at these goals, there are three important principles to remember as you approach the small group meeting.

**1. GUIDING IS MORE IMPORTANT THAN RESOLVING.** As a small group leader, it's tempting to try to resolve issues or answer questions for students; but it's more effective to guide them in their own spiritual growth. This means paying attention to how kids think, process, and respond—not doing it for them. Don't feel like you have to have everything wrapped up at the end of each meeting. The thinking that happens between meetings can produce the most growth.

**2. QUESTIONS ARE MORE IMPORTANT THAN ANSWERS.** Questions unlock secrets and dreams that lay hidden in the heart. That's what makes them so powerful. Through his questions, Jesus inspired people to receive healing they didn't know they needed, to confront struggles they didn't know they had, and to expose secrets they didn't know they kept. And he invites us to the same ministry.

Good questions guide, invite, reveal, and open us up. Bad questions direct, threaten, intimidate—they ultimately have the opposite effect. In the context of a small group meeting, a bad question causes kids to feel unsafe, to think there is only one "right" answer, or to believe they are required to offer an answer they are not yet ready to give. Be willing to revise or delete questions when necessary, and take great thought and care in deciding which questions to include in your small group.

> ## "SMALL GROUPS ARE MORE THAN JUST OPPORTUNITIES FOR YOU TO IMPART INFORMATION. THEY ALLOW KIDS TO EXPERIENCE CONNECTION IN A RELATIONALLY STARVED WORLD."

**3. LISTENING IS MORE IMPORTANT THAN TALKING.** Kids don't need another adult telling them what to do. They have plenty of those people in their lives already. What they need is someone who will listen—and that's a job description you can fulfill. Here is an acrostic that may be helpful in improving your listening skills:

Listen slowly: Take time to listen beneath and beyond the spoken words.

Invite: Use questions and allow periods of silence to leave room for students to talk.

Focus: Try not to be distracted; but if you are, schedule a time to talk with that student later.

Embrace: Accept what students share, even if you disapprove or feel uncomfortable.

Remember that students are always testing the waters for what is safe to share. The safer you make it, the more they'll share. The opposite is also true.

With these principles in mind, let's look at five goals to consider when you have your small group meeting.

## SMALL GROUP MEETING GUIDE

| Connecting | Did you connect with the kids? Did they connect with each other? |
|---|---|
| Introducing | Was the topic introduced at the right time and in the right way? |
| Interpreting | Was the topic discussed? Did it connect with where students were spiritually? |
| Applying | Was the topic personalized in the lives of the students in attendance? |
| Supporting | Does each student sense a commitment from the rest of the group—including the leader—apart from the regular youth group meeting? |

## CONNECTING

UCLA researchers believe people need eight to 10 meaningful touches a day just to stay sane. Yet people today are more isolated than ever before. Broken families, increased technology, and fluidity of neighborhoods are just a few of the reasons why small groups are more than just opportunities for you to impart information. They allow kids to experience connection in a relationally starved world.

Connecting falls under the larger goal of Community (which we'll discuss in more detail in chapter 4) but it can be defined as the ongoing relational touch of another person. Small groups provide a context for this to happen. Here are five ways to experience connection in your small group meeting:

1. Allow each person to share something from their world with the group. (One idea is to have each person share one highlight and one low point from their week.)

2. Highlight one group member each week and have them share "their story." (A little about their family, school, interests, relationships, and so on.)

3. Have group members share leadership duties by delegating assignments and responsibilities. (For example, have them take turns leading the group, ask them to organize a social activity, and so on.)

4. Set up ground rules for listening and respecting each other during the group. (You may want to give them a quick lesson on active listening, or go over the LIFE acrostic mentioned in principle number three earlier in this chapter.)

5. Set up weekly prayer partners in your group. (Switch prayer partners each week so your group stays connected with everyone in the group.)

## INTRODUCING

Introducing means not assuming kids know or understand what you are talking about. Introducing means taking the time to creatively and effectively bring the topic to the table. Often, kids don't understand the topic at the end of the meeting because we didn't effectively introduce it at the beginning. Here are a few ideas for how to introduce a topic in a creative and clear fashion:

1. Use an object lesson. (See *Everyday Object Lessons for Youth Groups* by Helen Musick and Duffy Robbins for ideas on how to do this.)

2. Have students do a reading or drama on the topic you are teaching. (See *Spontaneous Melodramas 1 and 2* by Doug Fields, Laurie Polich, and Duffy Robbins for ideas.)

3. Do *Lectio Divina* with your students to help them think or meditate more deeply about the passage. (This idea is discussed in more detail in chapter 6, Level 4.)

4. Do a tension getter to get students to think about the topic.

5. Show a video clip from a movie or television show that relates to your topic. (See *Videos that Teach 1 and 2* by Doug Fields and Eddie James for ideas.)

## INTERPRETING

Two questions are critical in regard to interpreting the topic. First—
*Have we done our homework on the subject?* This doesn't mean we
have to be experts or develop some kind of immovable agenda. It
means we have a basic understanding of what we're trying to help
our students understand. Here are some study aids we recommend for
leaders:

1. *An NIV or NRSV Study Bible:* These have built-in commentaries and concordances, as well as introductions to each book
in the Bible.

2. *MacBible Software:* Every word, every verse, every book is
easily found on your computer so you can cut and paste them into
your notes.

3. *Topical Bible:* Breaks the Bible up into themes and categories
to make research more efficient.

4. *BibleGateway.com:* Enter a passage reference or key word
to bring up Bible text in any one of a dozen translations. Then
click another link to read about the selected passage in the IVP
New Testament Commentaries. Most of the New Testament
books are in there.

5. *Google.com:* This is so simple that we almost forget it is
an available resource. Just type in the subject you want to research and up pop Web sites and sermons about your subject.
Download them for study and for extra reading material. (But
please give credit where credit is due if you use someone else's
hard work.)

The second question we want to consider is—*Are we willing to involve students in the interpreting process?* The best small group leader has a clear grasp of the topic but allows the group to come to their own understanding of the topic by guiding them from behind. You can do this by knowing what you want students to learn but staying open to the direction the group takes in getting there.

## APPLYING

Author John Drane says, "Today's Christians will be judged more on the quality of their Christianity than on the truth of their claims." In other words, what kids *do* with what they learn will matter more than what they *say*. We need to be committed to helping our students not just know the truth, but be transformed by it.

Application is when students live what they have learned during the small group meeting. Therefore, our job is to give students concrete steps to apply what they have learned. A challenge to apply spiritual truth will go a lot farther in students' lives than merely having them regurgitate information. If we want them to develop a faith that carries them past their teenage years, we must help them assimilate the lessons they learn.

Asking "So what?"—and then giving your students opportunities to apply the principles they've learned—will take your small group lesson out of the meeting and into their lives. (Chapters 4 through 8 are filled with ideas to help you accomplish this goal.)

## SUPPORTING

Small group leaders who take their call seriously will go with their students after the meeting ends. Not physically—but mentally, emotionally, and spiritually. They stay connected to their students between meetings. In a study of resilient children, kids who transcended difficult circumstances had one common factor—nonexploitive adults who walked alongside them as advocates, encouragers, and supporters. As a small group leader, you have an opportunity to be that adult. By walking alongside your students, you will help them be more confident in their lives and in their faith. It's also important to help kids establish bonds *with each other* in your small group. Bonds of support and commitment remind each student that they are not alone—their group is with them. When they face challenges during the week, someone will lift them up when they have fallen. This is what it means to become the Body of Christ.

Hopefully these goals will help you make the most of your small group meeting. But your small group ministry is much more than a meeting—and that's what the next five chapters are about.

# CHAPTER THREE
# SMALL GROUP MINISTRY

Effective small group leaders appreciate the uniqueness of each student's faith. They also recognize their small group is an ongoing ministry. Too often a small group is seen as just a meeting, with ministry happening only while students are there. But small group leaders are not bound by the limitations of a meeting. They assume pastoral roles in the lives of students by understanding their spiritual, relational, and developmental conditions outside the meeting.

Our "Small Group Ministry Matrix" is designed to help you meet the deeper needs of the students in your ministry. It's a resource that will help you take into account the whole student.

The matrix is built upon five long-range goals for growth: Community, Worship, Discipleship, Service, and Outreach. Because it is safe to assume kids are all over the map in each of these areas, we believe it's helpful to develop a multitiered approach to your ministry. This is accomplished by establishing and defining six levels within each of these key growth areas. While you have significant long-range goals you are trying to accomplish with your group, the idea here is to recognize that your students are progressing toward them at different rates.

## "WE SERVE A GOD WHO KNOWS AND VALUES EACH OF US, AND WE SHOULD REFLECT THAT KIND KIND OF CONNECTION WITH KIDS."

Each growth area outlined in the matrix has a goal and anchor verse, followed by six levels of increasing development. Before we dive in to the areas of growth and their corresponding levels, we want to suggest some principles you should think about as you're using this tool to develop your ministry.

**PRINCIPLE I:** *The matrix helps you realize the need to know your students.*

There are few things more valuable in ministry than knowing and understanding your students. We serve a God who knows and values each of us, and we should reflect that kind of connection with kids. The charts provide a way to help you discover and understand where your students are—developmentally, emotionally, and spiritually. The subsequent ideas and resources are designed to help you move beyond your meetings into a soul-connecting relationship with your kids.

**PRINCIPLE II:** *The levels serve as a direction not a formula.*

Our chief concern in writing this book was that readers would interpret the levels as "categories" to be used to label kids rather than processes that point them in good directions. The danger of any ministry resource is that it can become an imposed technique or formula. When this occurs, expectations replace understanding and performance begins to outweigh experience. We invite you to use the definitions and levels as a springboard for your own ideas about nurturing your students' growth. You know your kids best—and you know what will encourage them most. Our goal is that this matrix will assist you in the process.

**PRINCIPLE III:** *Your experience in one growth area will affect your experience in other growth areas.*

The discipleship journey is filled with encounters with worship, service, and outreach. Outreach and service bring life to discipleship. Worship is the love language of the disciple and becomes the experience and expression of Christian community. As students experience community, their desire to reach out to others will be inflamed. The combinations are endless and exciting. Our research with small group leaders showed this common thread: Experience and growth in one area has a direct impact on the others. As you evaluate where your students are, we encourage you to consider the connection between growth areas and how each level might impact the others. This will help you minister to your kids in a more holistic way.

**PRINCIPLE IV:** *Moving on to the next level doesn't mean you leave past levels behind.*

Remember that you take each level with you as you move on to the next one. While there is a component of increasing maturity, even the most mature student will continue to be dependent on previous levels. Helping the poor is meaningless and lonely without a consistent connection to the foundational truths of serving. For example, remembering our first love is the soul-restoring connection that moves us toward outreach and discipleship. When you are challenging students with the deeper disciplines of the faith, it doesn't mean you no longer need to laugh, have fun, or just hang out with your kids. The bottom line is that the matrix is not linear, it is fluid—and you will move up and down the charts throughout your small group ministry years.

**PRINCIPLE V:** *Your small group ministry will change your life, not just your students' lives.*

If some of the definitions on the matrix make you feel inadequate, unqualified, and ready for some monk or super-servant to take over your ministry, then you understand what ministry is all about! God uses ministry to change us—not just the students he entrusts to us. Many people think ministry is what God does through us. But it's also about what God wants to do in us. As you consider how to challenge your kids through the use of this matrix, our prayer is that it will have the side effect of drawing you into a deeper and more intimate relationship with Jesus.

## THE SMALL GROUP MATRIX

Here are the characteristics of the growth areas in the matrix, with goals and corresponding Scripture verses for each area

| | GOAL | ANCHOR VERSE |
|---|---|---|
| COMMUNITY | We desire to create an environment where students feel cared for and safe. We seek to establish trust and credibility and to earn the right to speak loving truth into their lives. | "As iron sharpens iron, so one man sharpens another" (Proverbs 27:17). |
| WORSHIP | We want to see God at the center of our students' lives. We believe God reveals himself to us through worship. Our desire is to expose students to the God who is not just a part of their lives, but is their lives. | "When they looked up, they saw no one except Jesus" (Matthew 17:8). |
| DISCIPLESHIP | We want to foster a passion in students to learn more about God and his Word. We desire to nurture transformational growth in their spiritual journeys—from where they are to where God wants to take them. | "Do not conform any longer to the pattern of this world, but be transformed by the renewing of your mind" (Romans 12:2). |
| SERVICE | We want our students to move to a place spiritually where they are living out their faith. We desire to see students become more like Christ by serving each other, the church, and the wider community—for we believe it's through service to others that our lives are changed. | "I'm telling the solemn truth: Whenever you did one of these things to someone overlooked or ignored, that was me—you did it to me. " (Matthew 25:40 The Message) |
| OUTREACH | We want to create a supportive environment where students are able to bring non-Christian students to hear the gospel message. We also want to equip them with the ability to share their own faith. Our desire is to foster a passion to share Christ. | "How beautiful are the feet of those who bring good news!" (Romans 10:15). |

# SMALL GROUP MATRIX (DEFINITION OF LEVELS)

Now let's take a look at how each of these levels is defined.

| | COMMUNITY | WORSHIP | DISCIPLESHIP | SERVICE | OUTREACH |
|---|---|---|---|---|---|
| LEVEL 1 | Getting students to show up and connect with each other. | Helping students see, feel, and experience God. | Sparking a spiritual interest in your students. | Exposing students to the needs of others. | Helping students discover they have something to share. |
| LEVEL 2 | Building mutual trust within the group in order to help relationships grow. | Introducing students to the concept of worship. | Introducing the spiritual disciplines (reading the Bible, prayer, and so on). | Introducing various service opportunities to your students. | Helping students find opportunities to connect with non-Christian friends. |
| LEVEL 3 | Inviting students to share their lives outside of the group. | Helping students recognize how God is working in their lives. | Helping students make a connection between the spiritual and their everyday life. | Helping students learn to serve within the church. | Committing to pray and care for friends and family of the other students in the group. |
| LEVEL 4 | Encouraging students to go deeper with each other personally and spiritually. | Giving students opportunities to experience intimacy with God. | Encouraging students in the ongoing practice of spiritual disciplines. | Helping students to recognize and meet other people's needs in everyday life. | Creating special small group activities to which students may invite their friends. |
| LEVEL 5 | Challenging students to support each other and hold each other accountable. | Helping students learn to practice worship as a lifestyle. | Helping students learn and work through the deeper truths of the faith. | Encouraging students to practice service as a lifestyle. | Helping students learn how to share the gospel. |
| LEVEL 6 | Looking for ways to expand your community. | Challenging students to depend on God and trust him at every turn. | Challenging students to share their lives and disciple others. | Challenging students to begin to lead others in service. | Helping students develop outreach opportunities within their circles of influence. |

In the following chapters, you will find ideas to help your group develop in these specific areas. Each activity should be chosen with discernment, and they each may need to be adapted to the particular needs of your group. Here is a tool to help you take inventory and make use of what you know about your students. It's called the Small Group Profile, and it will help you as you begin to navigate your direction with your small group.

# SMALL GROUP PROFILE

| NAME | |
| --- | --- |
| AGE/GRADE | |
| SPIRITUAL UNDERSTANDING | |
| FAMILY SITUATION | |
| CHURCH INVOLVEMENT | |
| INTERESTS/PASSIONS | |
| PERSONALITY TRAITS | |

| NAME | |
| --- | --- |
| AGE/GRADE | |
| SPIRITUAL UNDERSTANDING | |
| FAMILY SITUATION | |
| CHURCH INVOLVEMENT | |
| INTERESTS/PASSIONS | |
| PERSONALITY TRAITS | |

From *Small Group Strategies* by Laurie Polich and Charley Scandlyn. Permission to reproduce this page granted only for use in buyer's own youth group.This page can be downloaded from www.youthspecialties.com/store/downloads   password: smallgroup
Copyright © 2005 by Youth Specialties

# SMALL GROUP PROFILE

| NAME | |
| --- | --- |
| AGE/GRADE | |
| SPIRITUAL UNDERSTANDING | |
| FAMILY SITUATION | |
| CHURCH INVOLVEMENT | |
| INTERESTS/PASSIONS | |
| PERSONALITY TRAITS | |

| NAME | |
| --- | --- |
| AGE/GRADE | |
| SPIRITUAL UNDERSTANDING | |
| FAMILY SITUATION | |
| CHURCH INVOLVEMENT | |
| INTERESTS/PASSIONS | |
| PERSONALITY TRAITS | |

From *Small Group Strategies* by Laurie Polich and Charley Scandlyn. Permission to reproduce this page granted only for use in buyer's own youth group.This page can be downloaded from www.youthspecialties.com/store/downloads   password: smallgroup
Copyright © 2005 by Youth Specialties

After you have used the Small Group Profile to assess the students in your group, take some time to evaluate how your group fits into the Small Group Matrix. As you look at the goals for each level, you can determine approximately where your group fits in the areas of Community, Worship, Discipleship, Service, and Outreach. Circle the level that best defines your group. (Keep in mind that your group could be at a different level in each area—for example, Level 4 in community, but Level 2 in worship.)

## "GOD USES MINISTRY TO CHANGE US—NOT JUST THE STUDENTS HE ENTRUSTS TO US. MANY PEOPLE THINK MINISTRY IS WHAT GOD DOES THROUGH US. BUT IT'S ALSO ABOUT WHAT GOD WANTS TO DO IN US..."

This group evaluation will help you as you look at the ideas and activities in the following chapters and determine which ones will help you in your goal of spiritual growth. Remember that all the ideas and activities can be used at any level; we have simply categorized them so you can have a more purposeful approach in your small group ministry.

Ministry is never linear, and God works beyond our categories and definitions to meet kids in all ways, at all times. With that in mind, our hope is that these ideas and activities will aid, empower, and ignite your small group ministry.

# CHAPTER FOUR
# COMMUNITY

AS IRON SHARPENS IRON,
SO ONE MAN SHARPENS ANOTHER.
—PROVERBS 27:17

The goal for small group community is to create an environment where students feel cared for and safe, to establish trust and credibility, and to earn the right to speak loving truth into their lives. Here are some ideas for building community at each level of your small group.

## LEVEL 1: GETTING STUDENTS TO SHOW UP AND CONNECT WITH EACH OTHER.

1. Postcards, Pictures, and Personal Notes—Get a bunch of postcards, and in your spare moments at work or while watching TV at home, write each student a quick note. It could be just two sentences long, but it means a lot to a student to get something (other than junk mail) delivered to their door. Pictures can also be sent as postcards—as long as they are the same size as standard postcards—and that's a fun surprise for students to find in the mail. Add humorous captions encouraging them to show up at your group!

2. Phone Calls and E-mails—This seems obvious, but it's amazing how much students appreciate a phone call, even if it's just a few minutes long. If you don't have a lot of time, call while they're at school and leave a message letting them know that you're thinking about them and you hope to see them at your group. Most students communicate regularly by e-mail or instant message, so this is also great way to keep in contact and encourage them to come to small group.

3. M&M Sharing—Pass around a bag of M&Ms during your group and have each student grab one (or several). Then go around and have them share a specific thing according to the color of M&M they grabbed. These could be questions about their family, their interests, their week, and so on. Designate one question per color.

4. Toilet Paper Sharing—Have the kids take as many squares of t.p. as they would use (don't tell them why). Then for each square they take, they must share one thing about themselves (or about their week). Go around the group until the toilet paper is gone!

5. Share Questions—Cut up some share questions and put them in an envelope (or shoe box). Have each student draw a question and answer it; then they choose the next student who gets to share. You can keep the box and use it at the beginning of each meeting while your group is getting to know each other. (For help with questions, try *Small Group Qs: 600 Eye-Opening Questions for Deepening Community and Exploring Scripture* by Laurie Polich).

6. Cooperative Eating—This is a great hands-on activity (literally) for building closeness within your group. Sit your group around a table that's loaded with everything they need for a spaghetti lunch. Then tie the students' wrists together—binding each person to the students sitting on either side of them. Serve the spaghetti and tell them to start eating, but their wrists are still joined together, so they'll have to cooperate to do it. (This is a great time to take pictures!) After some time, tell them to stop feeding themselves and start feeding each other instead. It's a fun activity that makes the kids work together in a whole new way!

7. Who Belongs—Have each student come up with two lists: One is a list of all the people they belong to; the second is a list of all the people who belong to them. The lists are meant to help kids understand that they have a part in helping others feel welcome. Have a discussion about what makes *them* feel like they belong—and what they do to help *others* feel they belong. Discuss how you can apply those things to your group.

8. Where Do You Belong?—Have each student identify all the different places, clubs, groups, families, and communities they belong to. These are not individuals but the little communities—athletic teams, classes, neighborhoods, relatives, and so on. On a scale of 1-10, have the students rate the significance and impact these groups or teams or places have had on their lives and why. Discuss what you can do to make your group a significant place of belonging in their lives.

## LEVEL 2: BUILDING TRUST WITHIN THE GROUP FOR THE RELATIONSHIPS TO GROW.

9. Common Experience—Place large sheets of white paper on the wall, one for each person in the group. Have your students use them to list the top-10 experiences from their lives—positive or negative. Experiences could be a vacation, a broken arm, making the team, getting cut from the team, or a first date. Pick one or two students' lists to read out loud to the rest of the group. As you name each event or situation, ask the other students to raise their hands if they've also experienced it. Circle the ones that at least one other person in the room has in common with the list maker. Discuss the benefits of the common experience and how your small group can become a common experience for your students.

10. Rules of the Community—Have each student write down three rules for the small group on a piece of paper. They can range from funny ("Everyone must take a shower before the group") to serious ("Everything is kept confidential"). List all the rules on a large sheet of poster board and choose the top 10. Print them on small laminated cards and hand them out at the next meeting. Discuss the importance of being committed to the rules they have established for the group.

11. One-Word Sharing—Ask the kids to describe their week in one word, or ask them to share how they're feeling right now in one word.

They can't share more than that until after everyone else has shared their word. This helps students learn to use words to describe their feelings, and it also helps them begin to share their feelings with the group.

12. Highlight/Low Point (also known as Best and Worst)—Ask students to share the best and worst parts of their weeks and why. Establish a time limit and go around the group so each student has a chance to share. Discuss the characteristics of what makes something the best for them and what makes something the worst. Ask how each of you can be a "best part" for each other and how you can support each other when someone experiences a "worst part."

13. Two Truths and a Lie—Have students write two true things about themselves and one lie on index cards *without* their names (this can be anything from childhood memories to favorite movies, to crazy things they've done). Then take all the cards and read them one at a time. Have the students guess whose card it is and which statement on that card is the lie.

14. Share Dice—Make up cardboard dice that have a question or thought for sharing written on each side. (There should be a mixture of "surface-level" and "deep" sharing statements.) One student tosses the dice and answers whatever side comes up. Then that student gets to choose who shares next.

15. Baby Pictures—Have students bring in baby pictures or pictures from their childhood (sport team, class, family). Each person then shares the story behind the picture. Have them talk about what they were like as children as well as one thing they miss and one thing they don't miss from their childhood.

## LEVEL 3: INVITING STUDENTS TO SHARE THEIR LIVES INSIDE AND OUTSIDE OF THE GROUP.

16. Care Packages—Send a care package to one of your group members for a birthday, a special sports event, or during finals week. Include notes of encouragement, meaningful Scripture, and pictures of the group. (Candy, cookies, new pens, stickers, magazines, and so on are also welcome.) And remember that random items that represent inside jokes from your small group can really bring a care package to life.

17. Posters of Encouragement—Along the same lines as the care package idea, get together with some students and make huge posters on butcher paper or poster board and secretly place them on someone's room window or car. This is fun for birthdays, to say congratulations for an athletic victory, to say good luck for something big coming up, or even to say, "We've missed you!"

18. Sticky Note Challenge—Get a pack of those sticky notes and pass out 10 to 15 blank notes to each student. Challenge them over the next week to write encouraging notes to each group member and "sneak" them someplace where they will discover them—their lockers, on their Bibles, or in their rooms, for example. The next week you will have fun sharing where the students found their notes. We remember one guy who found his on the lid of his toilet seat. When he lifted up the seat, it read, "Hope everything comes out okay!"

19. Small Group Overnight—One way to strengthen relationships in your small group is to have an overnight—either at the church or at one of your student's houses. Great bonding can happen when students have an extended time to play games, watch movies, eat food, and hang out. It's also a great way to get to know the students' parents—especially if it's at their house! Be sure to bring a camera and send pictures to everyone after the event. This is a great way to start making memories with your group.

20. Who Are You?—Give the students index cards and have them answer the question, "Who are you?" in one paragraph. Then discuss the things they use to answer that question (in other words, the things they do, the way they look, what others say about them, and so on). This activity is a good lead-in for a discussion on identity and how we define ourselves. It also allows the small group to get to know each other better and deepen relationships.

21. Show & Tell Box—Take a shoe box and anoint it "The Official Small Group Box." Have a different student take The Box home each week. When that student comes back to small group, The Box should be filled with things that represent who they are (pictures, special memories, childhood toys, books, and so on). Give them 10 minutes at the beginning or end of your group time for Show & Tell. They should share what's in their boxes and why they chose the things they did.

22. Who You Are—Before your group begins, place a picture of each student on separate pieces of card-stock paper, leave enough room around the picture to write. During your group time, have a discussion about the definition of community (see Acts 2:42-47) and how each person in the group is a vital part of your small group community. Pass each picture-paper around and have students write a sentence about that person's strengths and what that person contributes to your community. Pass the picture-papers around a few times, if necessary. You can keep and post their pictures in one place, or give them their pictures to take home as a reminder that they are a significant member and contributor to your community.

## LEVEL 4: ENCOURAGING STUDENTS TO GO DEEPER WITH EACH OTHER PERSONALLY AND SPIRITUALLY.

23. A Hope and a Fear—Turn the lights off and light a candle. Give students the rule that the person holding the candle is the only one who can talk. Pass the candle around your small group circle and have each person share one hope and one fear. Pray for each student before the candle gets passed.

24. Collages—Have students cut out pictures and words from magazines and put them all together into one group collage to illustrate what they struggle with, what they're tempted by, what they want for their future, and so on. Make a color photocopy of the collage for each student to take home. You can also have students make an individual collage based on their own personal struggles, temptations, or fears. Use it as an activity to deepen the sharing.

25. Stories Connect Us—For this exercise you'll need a long roll of string or ribbon. Have everyone sit in a circle and think of a favorite childhood memory (or you could pick another topic like an embarrassing story, a fearful moment, and so on). As each student shares, she holds onto a piece of the string and then passes the rest of the string to a student across the circle. This goes on until every student has shared and is holding a piece of the string. By that point, there should be a web of string across the whole circle. You can talk about several things at this point: How we are connected by our stories, how the body of Christ is connected, and how our stories are connected to the gospel story.

26. Life Landscape—Give students paper and markers and have them each draw any landscape that they feel represents their lives. Have them add animals, plants, or objects that represent the people in their lives. For example, one student we know drew a desert with a fountain for her dad (because they are close) and a cactus for her mom (because they are not as close). Have each student share their landscape with the group.

Discuss where the small group fits in the landscape of their lives and how they can nurture their landscape.

27. Draw Your Home Life—Have students draw a bird's nest to represent their life at home. Then have them explain why they drew the picture the way they did. One student might draw a nest without birds to show that their family is never home; another might draw a nest that is falling apart to represent a broken home; or a third student might draw a nest that is filled with lots of baby birds to represent younger siblings, and so on. Use it as a springboard for deeper discussion about family issues.

28. Encouragement Cards on Rings—For this activity you need index cards and small metal rings (which you can buy at any stationary or drug store). Punch holes in the cards and on each ring put the same number of cards as you have students in your group. Each student writes their name on the front of their little packet of cards and then passes it around the circle. Everyone writes something they like about that student on one of the cards. (All the passing and writing goes on at the same time). Tell them to focus on a *character* quality, not something related to the person's appearance. You can share them out loud, or just give them to the students to take home after the group.

## LEVEL 5: CHALLENGING STUDENTS TO SUPPORT EACH OTHER AND HOLD EACH OTHER ACCOUNTABLE.

29. Group Encouragement—Put each student in the "hot seat" and have the other students tell that person what they like or admire about them. Remind them to say, "What I like about you…" instead of "What I like about *her*…" and tell them to focus on character qualities, not superficial things. Positive reinforcement can be the best way to hold someone accountable to living the way God wants us to live.

30. Love Languages—Discuss the various love languages that Gary

Chapman defines and describes in his book, *The Five Love Languages:* Encouraging Words, Quality Time, Physical Touch, Acts of Service, and Gifts. First, have your students identify their two primary love languages. Then ask them to identify the love language spoken by their family or friends and talk about how we all receive and express love in different ways. Help them see how we can better care for others by expressing our love using their primary language instead of our own. Challenge them to speak another person's language of love at least once in the week ahead. (Special Note: This exercise is especially helpful for you as a leader. Once you know your students' love languages, you can care for them more specifically and effectively.)

31. Crossing the Line—This is a great way to get students to start sharing their feelings and opinions—especially about lifestyle changes God may want them to make. First, use masking tape to create a line down the center of the room. One side of the tape represents an "I agree" response and the other side represents "I do not agree." Next, give each student a piece of paper and a pen, and then explain that they will answer each question or respond to each statement silently. Read off a list of choices, commandments, verses, and so on—one statement at a time. If they agree with what you read, they go to the "I agree" side of the tape, and vice versa. If they want to explain their choices or ask questions about that topic, then they should write down their question or comment and save it for the discussion to come. After you've gone through all the statements, sit down and talk about one or more of the issues that were raised and God's perspective on them. At this time students can ask each other why they each chose to stand on one side or the other. This can lead to a good time of sharing and accountability regarding students' choices outside of small group.

32. Write Your Epitaph—Ask the students to take a moment or two and write their own epitaph or obituary. This lends itself to a discussion about what *really* matters in life, what goals we should set, and

how we can live the way we want to be remembered. (It's better to look forward with promise than backward with regret.) Use this exercise as an opportunity to hold your students accountable to working toward the goals they have set for their lives.

33. The Bandages We Use—Get some butcher paper or a piece of poster board. Brainstorm with your students about the kind of wounds we get—break-ups, hurtful things people say, low self-esteem, and so on. Ask the students what personally hurts them and write those things on the paper. Then put a real sticky bandage over each word. Now write on each bandage a behavior we use to cover up our pain—drinking, putting others down, eating disorders, and so on. Talk about how bandages temporarily cover the pain, but they don't heal us. After this exercise, find a way to hold each other accountable to remove some of the "bandages" the members of the group are using and lean on each other for support instead.

34. Accountability Prayer Partners—Pair up your students and tell them to "check in" with their partners—be accountable and available to them—throughout the week. Have each student pray for their partner every day and contact them at least once during the week to find out how they are doing. Have them ask their partners how they can encourage or support them and also how they can continue to specifically pray for them.

35. The Morning After—If a student knows she has a challenge coming up—specifically one that may involve some temptation, like going to a party or out on a date—assign one or more students in your small group to call them the next day. Because the student knows he will be getting a follow-up call in the morning, then hopefully the thought of that phone call will positively affect the choices he makes the night before!

## LEVEL 6: LOOKING FOR WAYS TO EXPAND YOUR COMMUNITY.

36. The Empty Chair—To get your students excited about how God wants to expand your community, leave an empty chair when you meet. Explain to your students that they are to pray for the person who will soon fill that chair. Encourage your students to also pray specifically about inviting a friend to your small group. Once a person comes to "fill the chair," create another empty chair and start the process all over again. As your group expands, decide when it's time to split off and create two groups. This may not happen until the following year, but your group will have a tangible opportunity to see how God is expanding your small group community.

37. Theme Night—Create a fun theme night with your group. For example, you could do an '80s Night—come dressed up like it's the '80s, listen to '80s music, go bowling, and watch *Footloose.* Or you could do a dress-up dinner night or a movie-theme night. Use it as an opportunity for your students to invite one of their friends who could be interested in joining a small group. (Be sure you end the night with an invitation to the visitors to come to the regular small group meeting the following week.) As your group grows, split into two groups and have the students begin expanding their community.

38. On Campus Community—Have your small group regularly host a casual lunch on their campus. This is not meant to be a formal event, but an informal gathering that lets other students know that while the friendships in your small group are deep, they are not "closed." Two senior guys from one small group noticed a freshman who had no one to sit with during lunch. Instead, he walked in a circle around his lunch area and never stopped to eat. These seniors invited him to sit with them and told him if he ever needed someone to sit with, they would always be available.

39. Jesus in My Community—Discuss in your small group how Jesus made people feel like they belonged (he was accepting, loving, a good listener, always inviting, welcoming). Also discuss how he created a community for the disciples and for strangers (he was inclusive, stood up for the oppressed, he served others). List all the ideas for the group to see and have each person commit to doing one thing that week to extend the Christ-community into their world.

40. Small Group Family Night—The goal of this idea is to include your students' families in your small group experience. Invite all the families of the small group members to join your group for a barbecue. Bring pictures, videos, and mementos from any and all small group experiences you have had so far. Remind your students that they are the hosts and not the guests. Talk in advance about how they can make everyone feel comfortable and how they can create the atmosphere of belonging they already share. This can be a great witness to those students' families who aren't involved at the church. They might consider attending after this!

41. Bring a Friend Night—This is similar to the "empty chair" idea but a bit more deliberate. About once every six weeks, designate a specific night for each student in your small group to invite one friend to attend. Make it a visitor-friendly night—show a video clip, have a topical discussion, and create a group sharing time that is welcoming and non-threatening. Tell the visitors they are welcome to come again the next week. If your group starts to grow, consider how you will split off into two groups—making sure each student has at least one friend with them in their new group. The regular practice of having your students bring visitors to the group will keep your small group from becoming closed and ingrown, and in the process they'll also learn to become a more welcoming presence in their community.

# CHAPTER FIVE
# WORSHIP

**WHEN THEY LOOKED UP,
THEY SAW NO ONE
EXCEPT JESUS.
—MATTHEW 17:8**

Our goal is to see God at the center of our students' lives, and we believe God reveals himself through worship. When students move God from being just a part of their lives to being the center of their lives—their faith becomes real, deep, and lasting. On the Mount of Transfiguration, the disciples experienced the essence of worship. Here are some ideas for worship at every level of your small group.

## LEVEL 1: HELPING STUDENTS SEE, FEEL, AND EXPERIENCE GOD.

1. Picture of Christ—Because images of Christ often evoke feelings, you can use a picture of Jesus to ignite deeper conversation. Photocopy one of the classic drawings of Christ—such as Jesus calming the storm, Jesus feeding the multitude, or Jesus carrying the sheep—from a children's Bible or a piece of art by a well-known artist like Rembrandt. Or you may also choose to share a more contemporary rendering of Jesus. Show it to your students and ask them to reflect on the scene, the people, or the message that the picture communicates.

2. Scripture Dialogue—After choosing the Bible text you will use for the lesson, determine the number of reading parts in the text. For example, if you were teaching about the raising of Lazarus (John 11:1-44), you would have the following parts: Jesus, the disciples, Mary, Martha, and the narrator (the voice of John). Make as many copies of the text as there are characters in the narrative. Highlight each person's reading part. Have the cast stand up and read their parts.

3. Personalize a Passage—Invite students to read through a passage and then rewrite it, personalizing the Scripture for themselves.

(Note: This works best for passages that promise, exhort, command, rebuke, or teach. It would not be as effective an activity if you used narrative passages.)

Examples:

"For God so loved_____that he gave his one and only Son, that if *I* believe in him, *I* shall not perish but have eternal life." (John 3:16)

"I plead with_____and I plead with _____to agree with each other in the Lord." (Philippians 4:2)

"But I tell_____that anyone who looks at a woman lustfully has already committed adultery with her in his heart." (Matthew 5:28)

4. Symbols—Ask students to find objects that symbolize where they are in their relationships with God. (It could be something in or outside your church building, an item they have on their person, something they found in their food, and so on.) Then go around the group and ask everyone to share why they chose the objects they did. Tell students to place their objects somewhere in their room, locker, or car to remind them of God's presence in their lives.

5. Prayer Walk at the Park—Take a field trip to a park with a walking path. Give students numbered envelopes to open at different locations along the trail. (Number the envelopes according to the order in which you want them opened.) You can design any kind of prayer walk you want—put Bible verses in the envelopes, questions for them to think about, or prayers for them to meditate on.

6. Personal Mad-Lib Paraphrase—This paraphrase works kind of like the old mad-lib idea, and it's another way to personalize a passage.

Here's an example:

"Therefore,_____,
                              YOUR NAME

I tell you, do not worry about _____.
                                SOME THINGS THAT YOU'RE WORRIED ABOUT

Is not life more important than _____?
                                 SOME THINGS THAT YOU'RE WORRIED ABOUT

Look at _____.
         AN EXAMPLE OF GOD'S CARE AND PROVISION AS SEEN IN NATURE

Don't you think,_____,
                              YOUR NAME

that you are much more valued by God than they are?

Who of you by worrying can add _____
                                 MONEY, TIME, NEW CARS, BETTER GRADES...

_____to his life?"
...GOOD HEALTH, WHATEVER IT IS  YOU ARE WORRIED ABOUT

(from Matthew 6:25-27)

7. Complete the Sentence—After your small group Bible study, give the students index cards or sticky notes with incomplete phrases written on them, then ask them to fill in the blanks. Examples:

"Because of what I have heard tonight I will_____."

"If what God's Word says is true, then I need to _____."

"After what I've heard here I am thankful for _____."

Suggest to your students that they post the phrases on their bathroom mirrors so they can read them each morning before they go to school.

## LEVEL 2: INTRODUCING STUDENTS TO THE CONCEPT OF WORSHIP.

8. Votive Candle Cross—To teach your students about prayer, arrange some votive candles in the shape of a cross. Tell them that the horizontal side represents prayer requests and the vertical side represents praises or thanks to God. Go around the circle and have each person share one request and one praise. After someone shares, that person should light two candles—one on each side. In the end, turn off the room lights so students can see the entire cross lit up. After this experience, talk about how prayer is not just about requests, but it's also about praise. And when we offer both of these things to God, that's when we truly see Jesus' cross in our lives.

9. Guided Meditation—Ask everyone to close their eyes and let their imaginations go as you read aloud the following meditation exercise.

> ### The Soldier
> *Imagine you are a Roman soldier in Judea*
> *About the time that Jesus was born.*
> *You are a part of an occupation army*
> *Whose job is to keep peace in that tiny nation.*
>
> *One night you become homesick for your family in Rome.*
> *You go outside into the moonlight.*
> *You walk across a field to a nearby hill and climb the hill slowly.*
>
> *When you reach the top of the hill*
> *You look up into the star-studded sky.*
> *All of a sudden, something remarkable happens.*
> *Off in the distance, toward a small town called Bethlehem,*
> *You see an unusual star rising in the sky.*
> *As it rises, it grows brighter and brighter.*
> *Then something more remarkable happens.*

*As you gaze at the star, your homesickness disappears,*
*And a tremendous peace fills your soul*
*A peace unlike anything you've ever experienced in your life.*

*As you continue to gaze at the star, you can't help but think*
*That the peace you are experiencing*
*Has something to do with that star.*
*You wonder where the star came from and what it means.*

*Saint Matthew writes in his Gospel:*
*When Jesus was born ... magi from the east*
*Arrived in Jerusalem, saying,*
*"Where is the newborn king of the Jews?*
*We saw his star at its rising ..."*

*[The chief priests and the scribes] said ..."in Bethlehem ..."*
*[The magi] set out. And behold,*
*the star that they had seen at its rising*
*preceded them, until it came and stopped*
*over the place where the child was.*
*They were overjoyed ...*
*And on entering ...*
*They saw the child with Mary his mother.*
*(Matthew 2:1-2, 5, 9-11)*

*Now for the remaining two minutes, just remain standing there*
*on the hilltop gazing at the star and enjoying the peace it brings*
*to your restless heart.*

*(From Prayer Paths, by Mark Link, Tabor Publishing, 1990.)*

After a few minutes, invite students to reflect or share or journal about their meditation experience.

10. Ignatian Meditation—This idea is adapted from Ignatius of Loyola where the leader invites people to use their imaginations to recreate a story in Scripture. These kinds of exercises can even be used in a Bible study, a small group, or in a large group teaching time. If we can pass them on to the individuals in our small group, we help kids get face-to-face with Jesus. Here are four ways you can get your kids to engage with a passage:

> 1. *Go there!* Position yourself somewhere in the story. Where do you see yourself? Are you standing next to Jesus? Lying next to the lame man? Imagine you're right there observing the story as it unfolds...

> 2. *Be there!* Use the rest of your senses to experience the scene—touch, smell, listen, and feel.

> 3. *Become a character or an object in the story!* "How does the character feel?"

> 4. *Be you!* Enter the story as yourself: "How would you feel if you were there?"

Using the story of the woman who was caught in adultery from John 8, tell your students to approach this passage using one of the four ways listed above. Read John 8:3-11 aloud and then debrief with your group using these questions—

- What were you thinking or feeling?
- How would you have reacted to this situation?
- What do you want to say?
- What do you want to do?

Another way to use this idea is to have each student (or pair of students) reflect from the perspective of the three groups represented in the story:

- Person One—a Pharisee
- Person Two—the Adulterous Woman
- Person Three—someone in the crowd, maybe even one of the disciples

11. Quiet Time Tool—Paul says, "I press on toward maturity." He doesn't say glide, saunter, or walk. There is a sense of intentionality in his approach. Using the word *press* as an acrostic, here is a tool you can use in your small group or teach your students to use it on their own.

Pray: Ask God to prepare your heart for the time you are about to spend with him. This is a prayer of preparation—it could be a prayer of silence.

Read: Select a passage from Scripture and read it three times—first for content, second for meaning, and a third time for meditation. Meditation means staying with a thought long enough for the thought to make a difference. The idea here is to read the passage devotionally.

Examine: Ask yourself these three questions in regard to the passage: The idea now is to read for study—

- What does it say? (Information)
- What does it mean? (Interpretation)
- What does it mean for me? (Application)

Say: Write out or say out loud to God some of your thoughts and conclusions about how this passage will be lived out in your life today. You could journal here, too!

Share: Find two people with whom you can share what this experience has meant to you.

12. Worship Meditation with Song and Video—A great resource for worship media is Highway Video (www.highwayvideo.com). They offer quality videos you can play for your small group to help them experience a time of personal worship and meditation. Show your students the video, and when it ends, ask them to remain quiet while they either journal their thoughts or spend some time in silent prayer. You can also do this with a song or music video.

## LEVEL 3: HELPING STUDENTS RECOGNIZE HOW GOD IS WORKING IN THEIR LIVES.

13. Letters to God—Have your students write individual letters to God about whatever they want. Invite them to think about their lives and what experiences they would like to talk about with God. Then give them time to write letters that express any thoughts, feelings, and experiences they want to share with God (with the expectation that he will write them back).

14. Letters from God—Have your students choose some verses (from a list you construct in advance) and then use them to write personal letters *from* God *to* them (including promises, advice, and encouragement). This is a great way to help them view Scripture as a love letter from God.

15. God Sightings—Ask your students to keep a diary or journal of "God Sightings." When during the week did they notice God's

presence? When did they feel close to God—or far away from God? One idea is to have them keep journals in which they reflect for five minutes in the morning (*How do I expect God to show up today?*) and again in the evening (*How did God show up today?*). Then have them share their reflections during your small group time.

16. Questions for God—Have your students write questions they have for God—and why they have them. Keep a journal of these questions and periodically revisit them to see if the students' perspectives have changed and whether or not they still have the same questions.

17. Questions from God—These are questions God may have for your students! Ask your students to write down what they think God would ask them if they were face-to-face with him. This can be a great springboard into a discussion about God's character, his heart, and his perspective on the world and on us.

18. Real Life Art—Have each student take a blank piece of paper and some crayons. Give everyone three minutes to scribble on them in any way they like. Next have them rotate their papers in a circle until they see something in the scribbles that they can make into an actual drawing of some kind—something that is uniquely them—something that has to do with their life.

Then have them answer these four questions about their picture:

- What is the title of your picture?
- What is the subject of your picture?
- What is the effect or mood?
- What question is your picture asking?

What starts out as a fun time of scribbling can turn into a more meaningful encounter with God.

19. Diamond Prayer—The diamond prayer is an exercise designed to help kids look back on God's faithfulness in their lives. By filling in the answers to the questions below, they get to relive how *God poured out his Spirit* in a seemingly impossible situation.

ONE WORD: A SEEMINGLY IMPOSSIBLE SITUATION YOU'VE FACED.

———————

TWO WORDS: ADJECTIVES THAT DESCRIBE THE SITUATION.

———————————

THREE WORDS: ABOUT YOU OR AN ACTION YOU TOOK.

————————————————

FOUR WORDS: ABOUT WHAT YOU WANTED TO HAPPEN.

———————————————————————

FIVE WORDS: GOD POURS OUT HIS SPIRIT.

——————————————————————————————————

FOUR WORDS: ABOUT GOD OR AN ACTION HE TOOK—
MARKING THE TURNING POINT FOR THE BETTER.

———————————————————————

THREE WORDS: ABOUT YOU OR AN ACTION YOU TOOK.

————————————————

TWO WORDS: ADJECTIVES THAT DESCRIBE THE SITUATION OR
HOW YOU FELT ABOUT THE SITUATION.

———————————

ONE WORD: THE OPPOSITE OF THE WORD USED AT THE TOP.

———————

From *Small Group Strategies* by Laurie Polich and Charley Scandlyn. Permission to reproduce this page granted only for use in buyer's own youth group. This page can be downloaded from www.youthspecialties.com/store/downloads   password: smallgroup
Copyright © 2005 by Youth Specialties

Write only the words from the exercise to create a diamond shape

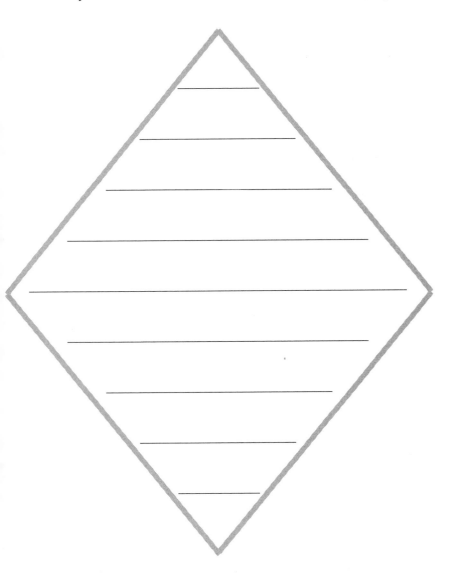

From *Small Group Strategies* by Laurie Polich and Charley Scandlyn. Permission to reproduce this page granted only for use in buyer's own youth group. This page can be downloaded from www.youthspecialties.com/store/downloads   password: smallgroup
Copyright © 2005 by Youth Specialties

## LEVEL 4: GIVING STUDENTS OPPORTUNITIES TO EXPERIENCE INTIMACY WITH GOD.

20. Prayers of Becoming—More than anything else, this generation of youth possesses a longing to *become* the kind of people God wants them to be. We've expanded the traditional ACTS prayer (see chapter 6) to represent four kinds of "prayers of becoming" for you to teach to your students.

> **A IS FOR ASPIRATION**—Focus on the quality of who I want to become—a prayer for Christ-like character. Aspiration refers to praying that we might become more like what God would have us to be, as in, "Lord, help me to be more loving." The focus is discipleship, to be more Christ-like.

> **C IS FOR COMMITMENT**—Focus on what I am willing to do—a prayer for Godly choices. Commitment refers to dedicating ourselves to new attitudes and behaviors that go beyond what we have been in the past, as in, "Lord, I commit myself to—helping the poor, being a servant, caring for others." The focus here is accountability to God for our spiritual growth.

> **T IS FOR TEMPERANCE**—(Note: This is not a word we use much, but it's one worth teaching to our kids.) Focus on what I am willing to give up or moderate—a prayer for balance in an unbalanced world. Where is your life "out of line"? Some youth workers I meet are the most stressed-out people I know. I don't think that's the way we should be!

> **S IS FOR SUBMISSION**—A prayer acknowledging the Lordship of Christ. Even though submission can carry a negative undertone, it's a wonderful thing to submit to a God who has our lives in his hands anyway! Submission refers to opening ourselves to receive what God would have for us, as in "Thy will be done."

This may be the hardest prayer to pray because it means total submission to God's will!

21. Altar Prayers—Altar prayers are when we literally bring our cares and concerns to the altar. We can do this through written notes hammered to a cross or by inviting your group to kneel at a makeshift altar (which you have prepared beforehand) to pray and meditate.

22. Cross of Brokenness—Start by taking pottery or clay slates and breaking them into pieces large enough for students to write on. Give each student a broken piece and a Sharpie marker to write his or her name on one side and the things they need to be "broken of" on the back. Then, during a time of worship and reflection, have students glue their broken pieces of pottery to a cross with tile glue. One idea is to spread the putty over the things they need to be broken over and say, "These things have been covered over with God's forgiveness." Then have them glue the pieces to the cross. In the end a cross of brokenness is created with each individual's name displayed in a mosaic of tiles, yet only the individual know what they glued to the cross.

23. Bags of Sin—To help kids understand how unconfessed sin can begin to affect our spiritual lives, all you need is a table lamp (without a shade), several paper lunch bags, and a felt marker. As you shine the table lamp for all to see, discuss the nature of light and illumination, especially regarding spiritual light. Now write the name of a common sin—such as gossip—on one of the lunch sacks. Place the sack over the light. Now add more sacks—each labeled with a different sin, which the kids can suggest to you as you talk. Soon the light will be just a glimmer through its many coverings. Now pull the bags off one by one to represent confession and forgiveness—and the light shines brightly once again. (This idea was taken from *Kickstarters*, by Rick Bundschuh and Tom Finley, Youth Specialties)

24. Candle Sharing—Pass a candle around the room and let students share about some tangible and specific commitment they've made based on what they heard in this week's study. Close with a word of prayer that they will take this light out into the world. This is a simple exercise, but you can do it each week as a reminder to students that God wants to be a part of their lives after they leave small group.

25. Discipline of Silence—You can do this for 15 minutes, an hour, or part of a day—depending on your group. If you do it during your small group time, invite students to go to a place outside the room, house, or church and spend the time alone. You can give them questions to think about, Scripture verses to look up, or a blank sheet of paper to write whatever they want during this time. At the end of the period of silence, have your students come together and share about their experience. Whenever you feel your students are ready, you can do this for a longer period of time while on a retreat. It's amazing what students can learn and hear and experience when they take time to "Be still and know that I am God."

## LEVEL 5: HELPING STUDENTS LEARN TO PRACTICE WORSHIP AS A LIFESTYLE.

26. Index Card Reminder—This is a quick and easy exercise you can do with your students each time you meet. Have your students each choose one verse that stood out to them from the day's lesson and write it down. Then have them each write a two- to three-sentence prayer about how they want to remember the verse or put it into action. Have them each keep the card in their Bible, by their bed, or taped to their locker and meditate on it every day. You can even hold a contest to see how many students memorize their verses each week. Holding Scripture in your mind and heart is a great way to worship God.

27. Labyrinth—A labyrinth is a prayer exercise that takes your students through different stations as they meditate and worship God. You can find out more about this worship experience at www.proost. co.uk. There is even an interactive online Labyrinth that students can do on their own.

28. Washing Feet—One way to worship God is to do something Jesus *did*. (You will need tubs, washcloths, and towels for this exercise.) Read the account of how Jesus washed his disciples' feet (John 13). Explain to the group that they are now going to wash each other's feet. Put on some music, if possible, and then one by one each student should wash another student's feet. (If there are some problems between some of the group members, talk about forgiveness first. Then pair off the students who are at odds and ask them to wash each other's feet.) Afterward discuss how they felt. If they feel uncomfortable, talk about how the disciples may have felt and what it means to bring our relationship with God into our relationships with others.

29. Jesus Prom—Another way to put worship into action is to do something that Jesus *would do*. One example: A youth group decided to put on a prom for handicapped kids and adults—people who never got to go to the prom when they were teenagers. Following Matthew 22:1-10, this became the banquet for those who didn't get invited to the first one. It may be strange to think of a dance as a worship experience, but it was one prom where everyone felt the presence of God. On a smaller scale, this can be done with any school experience that tends to be exclusive or leaves out some students (a school dance, a party, an athletic event, an award ceremony). Have your small group recreate the experience and invite students who normally get left out.

30. Peanut Butter and Jelly—This is a service idea done in a worshipful way. A church dedicated a whole Sunday morning to the topic of service by carrying that theme throughout the message and the worship

time. After the service ended, they invited students to each make one peanut butter and jelly sandwich. While making the sandwich, the kids were asked to think and pray for the homeless person who would receive it, to imagine what it would mean for them to get a meal that day, and to reflect on how the person who would eat their sandwich is a part of God's kingdom. The students then delivered the sandwiches—and when they gave their lunches away, they knew that person had been prayed for and committed to the Lord. It was a tangible way for them to take their worship to the streets.

31. Unique Leaves—Pass out leaves to each of your students. Have them study their leaves and compare them to the other leaves in the group. Pass out construction paper, glue, and pens. Have your students glue their leaves onto the top half of their sheets, then write (also on the top half) how their leaves compare to the other students' leaves (greener, bigger, smaller, shaped differently, and so on). On the bottom half of the paper, they should write about the things that distinguish them from other students (things they're good at, talents they have, gifts they have been given, experiences they've had). This is a great way for students to see how unique God has made them—they are unlike anyone else on the face of the earth! And in that light, they should think about how God wants to use them.

At the end of your group time, have your students write down three to five ways their lives could reflect God's presence. What could they do with some of the gifts he's given to them? How might God use them, if they made themselves available? This could also lead into a discussion of the Vine and the Branches (John 15) and how we need to stay connected to the Vine (Jesus) in order to be used by God. Once leaves are removed from the tree, they wither and die. The same thing happens to us if we don't stay connected to Jesus.

## LEVEL 6: CHALLENGING STUDENTS TO DEPEND ON GOD AND TRUST HIM AT EVERY TURN.

32. Everyday Symbols—Let students creatively use inanimate objects (paper clips, paper cups, pipe cleaners, pieces of paper) to symbolize their responses to some truth you have discussed in this week's lesson.

- Let students brainstorm ways they could obey this truth, and then ask them to choose one way by doing something creative with their objects.
- Make a list of ways students might respond to a truth and then ask them to circle two to three on the list.
- Invite students to tell one another what decisions they've made and invite them to pray together.
- Invite students to publicly share their commitment with the rest of the group.
- Ask students, "What would this truth 'look like' if you applied it in your life tomorrow?" Again, have students creatively use their inanimate objects to symbolize their truth application.
- Ask students to brainstorm how the truth would look if they applied it in any or all of these five arenas of their life— school, family, church, inner life, relationships.

33. Clay in the Potter's Hands—For this exercise, you will need two lumps of clay; freeze one of the lumps before your small group meeting. Begin your group time by reading Isaiah 64:8. Pass around the two lumps and let students feel both of them. One will be pliable in their hands; the other will be hard as a rock. Have them reflect on which lump of clay best represents them—are they moldable in God's hands or impossible to mold? Are they somewhere in between?

Have them use this tangiable exercise as a springboard into a discussion about how much of their lives they've given to God's control—and how much they are resisting God. You can also lead into a discussion about the reasons we harden our hearts to God—lack of trust, fear of where he'll lead us, holding on to sin, wanting to control our own lives, and so on. Staying moldable is one way we can worship God throughout our lives.

34. Everything I Need to Know I Learned in Romans 12—Make copies of Romans chapter 12 and pass them out to your group. Read the passage out loud and tell your group that every time you read a commandment or challenge to live a life of worship, they are to yell out, "STOP!" The person who yells stop has to repeat the word or phrase and what they think it means. Take a moment for students to jot down notes, if they want, then move on. At the end of the exercise, have students circle the top-three challenges they have the hardest time living out. Encourage them to turn it into a worship experience this week—every time they are faced with one of these challenges, they have to stop, pray, and acknowledge God's presence. The next week have students share what their experiences were like (even if they failed) and what they learned about their relationship with God in the process.

35. Bind These Truths—Before your small group, get a variety of temporary tattoos of pictures or words for the students to choose. At the end of your group time, read Deuteronomy 6:4-9. After Moses shared God's commands with the Israelites, he instructed them to "bind the commandments on their foreheads." Tell your group that you are now going to do the same thing by putting a tattoo on their foreheads to symbolize things they need to remember about God from today's lesson. Encourage them to leave them on as long as they can so they will serve as reminders that they are "set apart" by God to worship and serve him.

36. Mirrors of God's Reflection—Pass out a small mirror to each member of your group. Next, read through James 1:22-25. In it, James says that those who merely listen to the Word and do not do what it says are

like people who look in the mirror and then turn away, immediately forgetting what they look like. Have your students take small sticky notes and each write one word or phrase that reminds them of one way they "forget God" (the Internet, certain personal relationships, TV, sports, and so on. They can write on as many notes as they want). Then have them place the sticky notes on the mirrors you gave to them.

As they notice how "covered up" their reflection is, tell them that their life goal as Christians is to remove the things that keep them feeling distant from God. Ultimately believers with these kinds of "distractions" in their life cannot serve as clear reflections of God to the people around them. But an uncovered mirror symbolizes how God wants them to live—focused on him.

# CHAPTER SIX

# DISCIPLESHIP

DO NOT CONFORM ANY LONGER
TO THE PATTERN OF THIS WORLD,
BUT BE TRANSFORMED
BY THE RENEWING OF YOUR MIND.
—ROMANS 12:2

The goal for small group discipleship is to foster a passion in students to learn more about God and his Word. We also want to nurture transformational growth in their spiritual journeys. Here are some ideas for how you can nurture discipleship at each level of your small group.

## LEVEL 1: SPARKING A SPIRITUAL INTEREST IN YOUR STUDENTS.

1. Surveys—Take a survey of what your students want to study in small group. You can make a list of Bible passages or topics and have them vote on them, or just have them write on index cards some of the topics they want to study.

2. What Kind of Lamp Are You?—Ask each student to describe his or her relationship with God as if it were a lamp. Examples: a broken lamp (used to work but doesn't anymore), a bright flashlight (shines brightly in the dark), a strobe light (on again, off again), a dimly lit floor lamp (consistent, but not strong), and so on. Have them explain why their lamps describe them and what they need to do to "fix" their lamps. You could also incorporate Scripture about Jesus being the light of the world and how we need to walk in the light.

3. Question Bowl—After reading a passage of Scripture, have each student write an anonymous question on a slip of paper. Put the questions in a bowl and pull out one question at a time. Ask students to come up with the best answer they can for each one you read. If you still have something to add, share your thoughts and then draw the next question.

4. Pictionary/Cranium/Balderdash/Taboo/Catch Phrase—In general these are fun games to play, but try playing them with a twist—plant secret additions to the cards before the game. For example, add words that are straight from school (like *drama, freshmen, prom,* and so on)

or from the teenage years (like *puberty*, the names of students' boy-friends or girlfriends, memories they have, or inside jokes). With the Cranium game you can have players try to create these words using the clay that comes with the game.

5. Songs of Love—Ask the students to brainstorm a list of songs they know that describe love. Together, discuss the lyrics and whether or not the lyrics are referring to God's kind of love. (You can also make this a "homework" assignment—have them choose songs and bring the lyrics to your next small group meeting.)

6. Videos That Teach—Showing video clips that convey or illustrate some kind of spiritual lesson is a great way to spark a spiritual interest in your students. Two books by Doug Fields and Eddie James, *Videos That Teach 1 and 2*, are filled with movie segments you can use, as well as questions and Bible verses to help guide your discussion.

## LEVEL 2: INTRODUCING THE SPIRITUAL DISCIPLINES (THE BIBLE, PRAYER, ETC).

7. Journaling—This is a great way for students to reflect on their lives and pray without being distracted. It can also be a way for students to take notes in small group or record prayer requests. You could incorporate journaling into your small group by buying blank notebooks, stickers, magazines to cut out, and so on. Give your students the notebooks and other supplies and let them decorate their journals. Hold onto them for your students so they can add to them each week. This is a great way to get this discipline started in their everyday lives.

8. Prayer Drawing—Have all your students write at least one prayer request on individual slips of paper and place them all in a jar. Each student then draws a slip from the jar and prays for that prayer request right then. This is a great way to start praying as a group, and it also

helps students get more comfortable with the idea of regularly praying for each other.

9. A.C.T.S. Prayer—As the leader, you will lead them through these four different kinds of prayer:

**A**doration—Praising God for who he is, not necessarily the things we're thankful for—that comes later.

**C**onfession—Keep these to one sentence at first—or even one word— because it can be intimidating to confess our sins out loud.

**T**hanksgiving—What we're thankful for.

**S**upplication—Prayer requests.

As you pray, you can say a few words to help usher the group into the next phase. For example, "God, now we want to confess to you the ways we have fallen short this week. I confess my pride..." and so on.

10. Individual Prayer Jars—Get some clay and have students design a bowl or jar. (Or you can also take the easy route and just buy some.) Hand out small pieces of paper so the students can write down their prayer requests and put them in their own jar. Each week during your small group time, have students look through last week's requests and remove the ones God has answered. This will give students a visual reminder of how God answers prayer.

11. Prayer Candle—Some students will really get into this—especially if they like creating a different atmosphere when they spend time with God. At the end of small group, hand out pillar candles to each of your students and tell them they can only light their candles when they spend time reading their Bible or praying. Make it a goal for students to "burn

down their candles"—it means they are spending time with God!

12. O.I.A. Bible Studies—Here's one way to help your students learn how to study the Bible. Divide a sheet of paper into three columns and write the following words—one word above each column—*Observation, Interpretation, Application.* Read through a passage of Scripture and—

a. Make observations about the passage—*What do I notice about this passage?*

b. Interpret those observations—*What do those observations mean to me?*

c. Brainstorm ways this passage applies to your life—*How can I apply this to my real life now?*

13. Work through a Devotional—There are a lot of student devotionals today. Find one that is appropriate for your students and try working through it together. Or you can distribute them as tools for their personal quiet times. Some good resources like *Youth Walk* (a monthly devotional for students), *Everything Counts* (a student adaptation of *My Utmost for His Highest*), and *Devotion* by Mike Yaconelli (offering a fresh look at following Jesus) are all available at www.youthspecialties.com. If your students would like to work through a particular book in the Bible, try these devotionals by Laurie Polich: *Dive into Living Water: 50 Devotions for Teens on the Gospel of John* and *I Am Not Ashamed: 50 Devotions for Teens on Romans* (both are available at www.abingdonpress.com).

## LEVEL 3: HELPING STUDENTS MAKE A CONNECTION BETWEEN THE SPIRITUAL AND EVERYDAY LIFE.

14. Closet Cleanout—Hold your next small group in front of the closet of one of your students. The messier the closet the better! (Make sure they have agreed to this exercise beforehand!) The student then invites his small group to help him simplify his life by cleaning out and paring down the clutter that has collected there. The exercise could last five (or 45) minutes. You can streamline the process by taking sections at a time—old shoes, clothes, keepsake boxes, other boxes, and so on. Let the students voice their opinions, but the closet owner has the final say. If something meaningful comes to the surface, allow the group to process the experience. Take time afterward to talk about the things that clutter our lives and why Jesus invites us to lives of clearing some things out in order to simplify. (We recommend reading Richard Foster's *Freedom of Simplicity*.)

15. Life-Verse Exercise—Have each student choose five life-verses from Scripture and share how these themes could be lived out in their lives. Introduce life themes of serving, being teachable, caring for the poor, or knowing Christ. Talk about the characteristics of a theme verse. For example, big enough to give your life to, captures what you would like to be known for, or gives you something to aspire to. Invite them to select one theme verse for the month and how that theme will affect their lives. Later, type up everyone's life-verses and hand out copies of the list at your next small group meeting.

16. Go Bury What You're Leaving Behind—All you need is a good spot to have a burial, a shovel, and some pieces of paper. Have each person share one thing they would like to let go of or leave behind. Then have them each write it down on a piece of paper. After you discuss these things (optional), go somewhere and bury the papers as a symbol of leaving them behind. (You can also bury them in a large flowerpot.) Together, pray that God will help you let go of those things.

17. Post Your Change—On big sheets of paper, write some topic headings—school, family, relationship with God, myself, friends, my time, and so on—then tape the sheets on the walls around the room. Give each person a stack of sticky notes and some silent time to write a sticky note that says what they would change for each topic. Then have them attach the sticky notes to the wall under the correct heading. This is a great conversation starter for your small group time, focusing around the idea that God wants us to make changes in all areas of life in order to reflect his presence (Romans 12:1,2).

18. Magazine People versus Real People—Round up old copies of fitness, muscle, or beauty magazines and have students cut out pictures of people they think fit the stereotype of the perfect man or woman. Together, discuss the world's ideal of success, beauty, and approval. Have each person share what cultural expectation is hardest for them to wrestle with and why. Discuss God's idea of beauty and have each person share one example of someone who is *truly* successful and beautiful by God's definition.

19. Guests—Have different people in your church (volunteer leaders, staff, or members of the congregation) come share their testimony with your small group. Invite them to share how they bring their relationships with God into their everyday lives—outside of church. The value to this exercise is that 1) students get to hear another Christian voice in addition to yours; 2) your students are exposed to different experiences than the ones you've had; and 3) the adult guest speaker gets to know your students better and can later recognize and be friendly toward them at church.

20. Real-Life Scenarios—Come up with some real-life scenarios (family fight, relational break-up, cheating in class, hostility, alcohol at a party), write them on pieces of paper, and put each scenario in a different envelope. During your small group time, grab an envelope

out of the pile, read the chosen scenario out loud, and then discuss what you probably *would* do in that scenario versus what you really *should* do. You can also do this by dividing the group into pairs and have each pair discuss a different situation and then share their responses with the group. This is a good way to discuss parental conflicts, dealing with guys (or girls), or difficulties with friends. You can also have students write out their own scenarios.

## LEVEL 4: ENCOURAGING STUDENTS IN THE ONGOING PRACTICE OF THE SPIRITUAL DISCIPLINES.

21. Practice Practical Spiritual Disciplines—Take the fruits of the spirit and brainstorm some everyday exercises that might develop that characteristic in the life of each student. For instance, to develop patience—for the next week students should purposely choose to get in the longest line wherever they go. For kindness—challenge them to choose the most "hard to love" person in their lives, and each day they are to do some kind deed or service for that person. For peace or joy—assign them one children's game (hopscotch, tag, hide-and-seek) to play every day. Have the group report the next week about their experiences.

22. My Heart, Christ's Home—Robert Boyd Munger's book is a fast, easy read with great ideas for discussion. Introduce the idea of the Holy Spirit dwelling within us and then discuss each "room" God enters. Have students discuss and write the names of those rooms that are the hardest for them to invite God to enter (the bedroom, the computer room, whatever it may be). Also, have them identify their "hall closet"—that place that hides the dark secrets, bad habits, and painful experiences that are the most difficult to turn over to God.

Optional idea: Make up keys for each small group member and have them "turn over the key" to their closet to you whenever they are ready to let Christ in. This can be a meaningful symbolic activity for dealing with something that is a deep struggle in their lives.

23. Celebration of Discipline—Read through Richard Foster's book *Celebration of Discipline* and choose one discipline per week (or month) that you want to practice as a group. This will help your students understand the value of spiritual disciplines by giving them a chance to practice and discuss them in your small group.

24. Lectio Divina—It means "sacred reading." *Lectio Divina* is a four-fold process of reading and praying Scripture that comes from the Benedictine Rule of Life.

> Step 1: Slowly read a short biblical passage aloud three to four times.
>
> Step 2: Meditate on the passage by listening for a word or phrase that seems to have special urgency. (Meditation is merely staying with a thought long enough for the thought to make a difference.)
>
> Step 3: Pray over the passage and ask God for guidance.
>
> Step 4: Contemplate the passage by listening for how the passage intersects with your life.
>
> Step 5 (optional): Write or discuss what God has taught you through this experience.

Invite your students to practice *Lectio Divina* in your small group, then challenge them to do it individually at least three times before you meet again.

25. Manuscript Studies of Scripture—Type out a passage of Scripture without any verse numbers or subtitles. Give students markers and have them individually read through the passage, marking it in as many ways as they can (writing down questions they have, circling words that are repeated, underlining sections they don't understand, drawing arrows between parts that are related, and so on). Discuss the passage and the things that stood out to them. This is a way for students to discover things in Scripture they hadn't thought of before, without the distraction of the verse numbers and paragraph breaks. It's also one way to get your students deeper into Scripture.

26. Solitude Meetings—This sounds like an oxymoron, but the idea is to help students discover and experience the spiritual benefits of solitude. As students enter the room, give them a short passage to read and instructions to find a quiet place to be alone for the first half of your meeting. They are not to do anything but sit in quiet thought and rest. You may give them some statements to use to direct their imagination, such as, "Imagine you are at rest with Jesus. Imagine the most serene and quiet place ever." At a certain time, invite them back to discuss their experiences. Was it long enough? Was it uncomfortable? How did God meet them in the stillness?

27. Day of Solitude—When your students are ready, carve out time to listen to God by taking them on a one-day "prayer and solitude retreat." In preparation for the day, consider some areas of struggle or any stress they are experiencing and where they would like God to meet them. Next, outline the day ahead of time so there is some structure to it, but be prepared to throw out the schedule if necessary.

The schedule may look something like this:

*Morning:* Silent walk with a friend (this will be the only time you are together until the end of the day) and then take a walk alone.

Possible activities during this time: Scripture reading, reflection, and meditation, journal response to the morning walk, reading, and reflection.

*Lunch:* Talk about the morning lessons and the issues that are troubling you. Listen to the still, small voice of God. Take a nap if necessary!

*Afternoon:* Take a walk with God and celebrate his creation and the life he has given you. Take inventory of your life—write down all the areas where God is present and where he doesn't seem present right now. Write down ways you can be more intentional about experiencing God's presence. Set goals or write a letter to God talking about the steps you will take to move toward him in each area of your life.

*Dinner:* Review your day over a reunion meal with the rest of the small group.

## LEVEL 5: HELPING STUDENTS LEARN AND WORK THROUGH THE DEEPER TRUTHS OF THE FAITH.

28. Mustard Seed of Faith—Read and talk about verses on faith. Buy a small bottle of mustard seed and show students how small a mustard seed really is. Have them each choose one thing in their lives that they think would be impossible without God. Give them each a bag of mustard seed and a little box (you can make the boxes together or buy them). Together, commit to putting one seed in the box every morning to remind yourselves to have faith in God that day and then pray for the impossible thing they mentioned. Check in with them the next week and ask if they remembered to do this each day.

29. Debates—To get your students thinking about both sides of a controversial issue, divide them into two groups. Select an issue (underage drinking, casual sex) and have one group come up with an argument for one side of it, while the other group comes up with the other side. Have them debate the issue (but don't allow just a few people to dominate the conversation). Now for the challenging part—tell them they have to *switch sides and argue for the opposite viewpoint.* You can do this with any number of issues—the idea is to get your students thinking critically from all sides.

Another idea is to have one team pretend they aren't Christians and argue about the reasons why they aren't. This will help your students think about how non-Christians view Christians and ignite a discussion about some of the objections to the Christian faith.

30. Spiritual Gifts—Look through the spiritual gifts listed in Romans 12 and 1 Corinthians 12. Now invite your students to take a spiritual gifts test. You can find a link to several on the Youth Specialties Web site (www.youthspecialties.com). These tests take a while, but you can ask your students to take the test at home, or allow some students to do parts of it during your group time over a period of weeks. After they've

taken it, you can discuss the results and the ways your students can use their gifts (especially within your ministry). Most students want to find out what they are good at doing and how God wants to use them. Finding and using their spiritual gift(s) will also help students grow in their faith.

31. Clay "Idols"—Read the Scripture about the idols we have in our lives, then give students some time to work individually and make a clay symbol of the idols in their lives (for example, a clock to represent busyness). Discuss those things and the power they have over us. Discuss the statement, "The way we define ourselves is our idol." Then have the kids smash their clay idols as a way of symbolizing their rejection of those things.

32. Beyond Balance Inventory—This is an opportunity for students to do an exercise that comes from an early church father. Augustine suggests that a well-ordered heart consists of loving—

- The right thing
- To the right degree
- In the right way
- With the right kind of love

Have your students each write a sentence that describes every area of their lives that they love—I love getting good grades, I love dating, I love hanging out with my friends. Have them write as many sentences as possible. Using Augustine's guideline, invite each student to evaluate each of these areas—Is this dating relationship the right thing? To the right degree? With the right kind of love? and so on. Use the guideline to discuss how students can have a "well-ordered heart" in the areas that mean the most to them.

33. Reviewing Your Day Exercise—In his book, *The Life You've Always Wanted,* John Ortberg talks about reviewing your day with God. This is an exercise you can take your students through, and it encourages them to live out the deeper truths of the faith in their day-to-day lives.

1. Invite your students to close their eyes, be still for a moment, and to quiet their minds.

2. Acknowledge that Jesus is present. Invite him to teach your group.

3. Go back in your mind to when you first woke up. Watch that scene, as if on video. What does it lead you to pray for? Confidence? Courage? Patience? What other virtue comes to mind that you could pray for as a result of how your day started?

4. Continue through the day, going from scene to scene (prompt your students' memories by walking them through the various parts of their school day). As you reflect on each scene, some may be filled with gratitude, others with regret. Either silently or out loud, have your students speak directly to Jesus about this. Invite them to pray for those they may have met or encountered during the day.

5. End with a meditation on one life-lesson they may have learned from the day, and then thank god for his mercy and love.

## LEVEL 6: CHALLENGING STUDENTS TO SHARE THEIR LIVES AND DISCIPLE OTHERS.

34. Leadership Reflection—To help students discover what leadership is, have them answer the question: *Who in your life would you follow into battle?* Have them describe those peopls and why each of them would follow them. Then, as a group, come up with a list of qualities these people have. This is a good opener for various discussions on leadership—why people followed Jesus, why people follow other leaders, and most importantly, what kind of leaders your students want to become.

35. Light of the World—Have one student hold a lit candle and attempt to walk between two lines of other students who are trying to blow out the candle. (Re-light the candle whenever it does go out.) Then do a Bible study on Matthew 5:14-15 and what it means to be "the light of the world." Discuss the ways the world tries to blow out our light. Help them remember that in the game they just played, someone always stood by ready and waiting to re-light their candles. Discuss who God has put in their lives that helps re-light their candles—and also whose candle they can help re-light. This will show them how God is calling *them* to help support others in the faith.

36. Share Theme or Favorite Verses—Have each student choose three to five favorite verses from Scripture and share why they like them. Invite them to select one each that might be a theme verse for that month and how that theme might affect their lives. (You can do this at the beginning of each month to help students learn to apply the Word to their lives and become an example to others.) Later, type up the verses and give everyone a list of the group's favorite verses.

37. Spiritual Life Buddies—The idea here is to invite your students to be committed to each other's unique relationships with God. Have students write three things on an index card:

1. What they want their relationships with God to look like
2. Areas in need of spiritual or personal growth
3. Needs, fears, and anxieties

They should also include their names and their phone numbers or e-mail addresses.

Place the cards in a container of some kind and have everyone draw a card. Next, have each student commit to pray for their chosen person and their requests every day for the next seven days. Discuss how they can be an encouragement to their assigned person and when they will pray for them each day. Invite them to be creative with their card—like posting it on their mirror, in their car, or on a nightstand. Finally, they should each check in with their assigned person at least one time during the week. Give students the opportunity to either renew their commitments to each other every week or change partners so that students get in touch with each other's spiritual life.

38. Lead a Small Group Meeting—We all know we learn more about something when we have to teach it. This exercise also helps students appreciate what you do for them every week. Divide the group into pairs (preferably pairing up the more knowledgeable students with those who don't know as much, or pairing up students who don't know each other as well). Assign each pair a week for which they are responsible for leading your small group. Give them guidelines such as how long the meeting should be, how to select a topic or Scripture, and how to come up with a creative or interactive way to teach the lesson. Meet with the pair during the week to help them prepare and guide them regarding how to lead others.

39. Mentoring—Partner with another small group of younger students and commit to being their mentors or big brothers and big sisters. Begin by talking about what true leadership and servanthood means.

Emphasize the privilege of being a spiritual mentor. Remind them that the power is in the hands of the disciple, not the discipler. Next, hold a few joint meetings with the partnering group to get students comfortable with each other. Finally, invite them to freely call anyone in your group for help, guidance, support, and encouragement when they need it.

# CHAPTER SEVEN
# SERVICE

I'M TELLING THE SOLEMN TRUTH:
WHENEVER YOU DID ONE OF THESE THINGS
TO SOMEONE OVERLOOKED OR IGNORED,
THAT WAS ME—YOU DID IT TO ME.
—MATTHEW 25:40 (THE MESSAGE)

Our goal for service is to move our students to a place spiritually where they are living out their faith. We desire to see students become more like Christ by serving each other, the church, and the wider community—for we believe it's in service that our lives are changed. Jesus' statement in Matthew 25:40 was a radical one that underlines the importance of service. And our service comes out of our love for Jesus. Here are some ideas for service at each level of your small group.

## LEVEL 1: EXPOSING STUDENTS TO THE NEEDS OF OTHERS.

1. Pass Out Lunches to the Homeless—A fairly simple idea is to gather your small group and pack lunches to pass out in an area where there are homeless folks. Be sure you gather everyone together after the experience for some follow-up and debriefing. This is a simple idea for exposing your students to people who don't have the luxury of food at their fingertips.

2. Tour a Home for the Mentally or Physically Disabled—This is a great way to give kids some perspective. Call up a group home or institute near you and ask if you can bring in some students to take a tour of the facility. After you have walked through, gather them together for your small group meeting and debrief the experience together. Exposure is what leads kids to serve—so find out if there are any opportunities for your students to volunteer there, if they want to.

3. Tour a Children's Hospital—Once again, an opportunity for kids to see children who have life-threatening diseases or other severe handicaps. Exposure to others with severe needs helps jolt students out of their self-focused perspectives and softens their hearts toward meeting the needs of others. After your tour, try gathering your students right there in the hospital (in the lobby or even in the parking lot) for your small group time so they can be as close to the experience as possible.

4. Center for Student Missions—This is a great organization for exposing kids to the needs of the inner city. CSM has several locations throughout the United States and Canada, and they run weekend and weeklong trips that are fully staffed—all you have to do is go with your kids! Your students will experience everything from helping in a soup kitchen, to running an after-school program, to passing out meals to the homeless, to taking a prayer tour of the city. This is also an excellent way to get exposed to some of the inner-city ministries near your church. Check out www.csm.org for more information.

5. Mexicali Ministry—Specifically for the West Coast, this is a weeklong mission trip to Mexicali sponsored by Azusa Pacific University. It generally happens over spring break, and it's a great opportunity to expose kids to mission work in a fun, hands-on, experiential way. Contact Azusa Pacific University Mexicali Outreach for information: www.apu.edu/iom/mexout/

## LEVEL 2: INTRODUCING VARIOUS SERVICE OPPORTUNITIES TO YOUR STUDENTS.

6. Free Car Wash—Have your youth group organize a regular car wash (at a gas station, shopping center, or church parking lot), but instead of charging people, wash their vehicles for free. Make it clear that there are no strings attached. If people want to pay for the service, make it "donations only" and give the money to a charity that your youth group wants to sponsor.

7. Creative Canned Food Drives—Find an organization that collects food for needy families and have your youth group spend an afternoon collecting canned goods. Here are a couple ideas to make it fun:

• Divide the group into teams and send them into the neighborhood for a limited time (like an hour) and have them collect as many canned goods as they can. The team that collects the most wins. (You may want to have some kind of prize to add incentive.)

• Have a "Scavenger Food Hunt." Give kids a list of nonperishable food items that they need to find and bring back within a given time limit. But they can't buy them; other people must donate them. Each item can be worth points based on how difficult it was to find it. And the more of a particular item they bring back, the more points they get.

• Divide kids into different cars and have them draw for street names or areas of your town. Give them an hour to collect as many canned goods or other nonperishable foods as they can from residents living in the area they chose. The teams report back and weigh all the food they collected. The team with the most food (by weight) wins a prize; all the food is donated to the needy.

8. Habitat for Humanity—This is a great opportunity for students to serve in a hands-on physical way. Habitat for Humanity is located throughout the U.S., and it is a volunteer-led organization that builds houses for families. Your students can simply volunteer for the day—or longer—and they will be told what to do when they show up. A great hands-on service opportunity for kids.

9. Adopt a Room—This is a great variation on Rest Home ministry. There are hundreds, if not thousands, of senior citizens in these homes who don't have a single visitor. Go to a local rest home or assisted living care facility and ask the front desk for the name of a resident who doesn't get many visitors. "Adopt" that person as your grandparent—visiting them once every week or two and bringing them little gifts and notes. It's a much more personal way to care for an elderly person who needs the touch of Jesus.

10. One Life Revolution—World Vision has partnered with Youth Specialties to bring students an opportunity to help with the AIDS crisis in Africa. Many different items can be donated to help the widows and orphans who are devastated by this disease. These items have ranged from $15 to $53,000—and your kids get to choose what they want to do with the money they raise. This is a great opportunity to do cross-cultural service in your small group. (See www.oneliferevolution.org for more details.)

## LEVEL 3: HELPING STUDENTS LEARN TO SERVE WITHIN THE CHURCH.

11. Secret Angel—Find a family in your church that is going through a severe illness or has experienced the death of a loved one. Make secret deliveries to their house—a hot meal, cookies, encouragement cards, flowers, Scripture verses, and so on. Sign your deliveries "Secret Angel." A great way to take advantage of Jesus' encouragement to do your act of service in secret—"But when you give to the needy, do not let your left hand know what your right hand is doing" (Matthew 6:3).

12. Help for the Elderly—Find a homebound person in your church and volunteer to work at that person's house for a day. The work could include gardening, cleaning, cooking, repairing—whatever needs to be done. (Don't forget that visitation is part of your ministry—many of these folks love to visit with students.)

13. Join a Ministry Team—Your students are not the church of tomorrow; they are the church of *today!* Encourage students to volunteer on Sundays at your church—working at the sound board, ushering during the service, passing out programs, cleaning up after the service, serving meals or snacks, helping with the parking ministry—all the same ministry opportunities that adults have in your church. One church we know of even had students on the building committee when they were

building a new sanctuary. There is no organ—but you should hear the sound system!

14. Work with Young Children—You'd be surprised how many high school and junior high students are great with little kids. And you probably *wouldn't* be surprised that your nursery or children's ministry needs volunteers! Have your students sign up once a month to serve in the nursery or in a children's Sunday school class during the worship service. It's a great help to parents—and fun for your students who like kids!

15. Create a Web site for Your Youth Ministry or Church—Youth today have so much training and knowledge about technology—why not have your kids volunteer to create and host a Web site for your church? Another way to use their technological skills is to create a tech team to support your worship services with media. Whether it's creating PowerPoint slides, running MediaShout (a high-end software, available through Youth Specialties), playing worship videos, or adding artistic creativity—your kids can serve the church doing what they do best.

## LEVEL 4: HELPING STUDENTS TO RECOGNIZE AND MEET NEEDS IN EVERYDAY LIFE.

16. Special Small Group Needs—This seems obvious, but the primary needs a small group should consider are the needs of those within the group! Periodically ask your students if anyone needs a little extra help from time to time (homework is overwhelming, chores piling up, special needs within their family, and so on). One member of a small group we know of got pregnant, so her small group spent the next nine months tending to her specific needs during that difficult time (see the full story in chapter 9). The baby was born healthy and given up for adoption, while the small group ended their service time to this girl by raising money for her to join a health club!

17. Newspaper Watch—Tell your group to watch the local newspaper throughout the week. They should look for stories about people who've experienced tragedies or who have special needs that the group might be able to meet. (Examples: A family's home was destroyed by a fire. Someone was injured in an accident.) List the needs and have your group answer the question, *What could we do to help?* Narrow it down to one or two crises that your group would be able to address the best, figure out what you could do to meet that family or person's needs, and then do it. This helps kids develop greater sensitivity to the news, and it makes them aware that real people and real lives are affected by what they hear and read in the media.

18. Rake and Run—Pile your group into a van or truck and cruise up and down the streets in your neighborhood looking for lawns that need raking. Have one member of the group go to the door of the house, knock, and then ask the person who lives there whether or not he wants his leaves raked. If he says yes, all the kids pile out of the van and rake the lawn and bag the leaves (with 8-10 kids, this should only take about 10 minutes). Let the homeowner know that this is being done for free. (Side Note: Remind your kids that they are on other people's property, and they should be careful not to damage anything through careless-ness or horsing around.) When the job is finished, your kids can leave a "calling card" from the youth group to let people know who they are and offer their best wishes.

Some other variations:

- Snow and Blow—shoveling snow off sidewalks
- Splash and Split—washing windows
- Mow and Blow—mowing lawns

19. Tutor a Child—Have your students volunteer a couple hours a week to tutor children in the inner city or your church—or even other

students their age who need help. (This could even be extended to students outside of your youth group—a great way to do outreach!) Have the kids in your group sign up, and then call a local agency (like some type of after-school program with the YMCA or an inner-city church) to find out if there are any children who need this kind of help. If you don't live near the inner city, you can find information through the Internet or even make an announcement in your congregation.

20. Thank You Officer—Police officers rarely receive thanks from the public. Have your group make a big sign or a bunch of cards, bake cookies or brownies, and then hit the police station around midnight when there is a shift change. (It's a good idea to warn them that you are coming.) Have your kids pass out the goodies to the officers and thank them for a job well done. (This can also be good PR if you plan on doing big, noisy outreach events in the future.) Consider doing this for your local firefighters, people who have served in the military, or other public employees as well.

21. Baby-Sitting Ministry—Many parents never get the chance to go out because they can't afford a baby sitter! Have your girls (or guys— not to be sexist!) create an advertisement for one free night of baby-sitting and pass them out in their neighborhoods. It's a great way for students to build relationships with families living around them, and it might even give them an opportunity to invite the families to church!

## LEVEL 5: ENCOURAGING STUDENTS TO PRACTICE SERVICE AS A LIFESTYLE.

22. Sponsor a Compassion Child—For $28 a month, your group can feed, clothe, and educate a child from a developing country and help her experience the love of Jesus Christ. Compassion International organizes their sponsorships so that your group can write to your child and get letters to you translated into English.

This is a tangible, ongoing way for your kids to experience the joy of giving. (Call Compassion International at 800-336-7676 or go to | www.compassion.com to learn more.)

23. Video Ministry—Make it a small group project to videotape the services of your church for the shut-ins and those who are ill or out of town. Your group can buy blank videocassettes, tape the services, and maintain the new video library, delivering videos to people who want to view the services. You can advertise in your church bulletin and have people call if they're interested. This would be a great ongoing service project for some of your kids to take on.

24. Inner-City VBS—Have your group conduct a Vacation Bible School for an inner-city neighborhood during the summer. There are usually hundreds of children in these areas. A VBS can be done in cooperation with an inner-city church that doesn't have the staff to sponsor one alone. Or you can rent a community hall or use a public park or some other location.

The best way to prepare for this is to involve your young people in a normal Vacation Bible School at your own church first. Usually preteens and teens aren't too excited about attending VBS, but if they know they are going to be putting one on themselves the following week, they will be more likely to take an active role in the first one—just so they can learn how it's done. This is also a good way for your children's minister to get some help from your youth group.

25. Be a Servant Week—This is a fun idea to make service more of an everyday activity. Distribute calendars for the week and have one act of service written on each day of the week. Example:

# BE A SERVANT WEEK

| | |
|---|---|
| MONDAY | Get the paper, make coffee, and bring it to your parents before they get out of bed. (If they don't drink coffee, bring orange juice.) |
| TUESDAY | Make your brother or sister's bed. (Wait until they're out of it.) |
| WEDNESDAY | Shine your dad's shoes. |
| THURSDAY | Make and serve dinner at your house. Serve the food, pour the drinks, and clean up the mess. (If you have a friend helping you, do the same thing at his house the following week.) |
| FRIDAY | Clean the kitchen. Clean behind the toaster and all those other places that don't get wiped clean very often. For an extra bonus, clean out the refrigerator—throw out those scary containers of food that have been there for a while. |
| SATURDAY | Kidnap a friend and take them to breakfast (on you!). |
| SUNDAY | Cook breakfast for your parents. Serve it to them in bed. (To make things easier, have them sleep in the kitchen.) |

(Adapted from Todd Temple's *How to Rearrange the World.*)

26. Servant Certificates—Pass out certificates for students to give to others as a promise to serve them. Give one to each student in your group each week or month, depending on what is realistic for your students. The point is to help them make service an ongoing lifestyle.

See the next page for a reproducable example!

# SERVING CERTIFICATE

"I,_____,

**STUDENT'S NAME**

PROMISE TO DO THE FOLLOWING ACT OF SERVICE:

_____

**WHAT YOU WILL DO**

FOR: _____

**PERSON'S NAME YOU ARE SERVING**

ON: _____

**THE DATE YOU WILL DO IT**

_____

**SIGNATURE**

From *Small Group Strategies* by Laurie Polich and Charley Scandlyn. Permission to reproduce this page granted only for use in buyer's own youth group.This page can be downloaded from www.youthspecialties.com/store/downloads   password: smallgroup
Copyright © 2005 by Youth Specialties

# SERVING CERTIFICATE

"I,_____,

**STUDENT'S NAME**

PROMISE TO DO THE FOLLOWING ACT OF SERVICE:

_____

**WHAT YOU WILL DO**

FOR: _____

**PERSON'S NAME YOU ARE SERVING**

ON: _____

**THE DATE YOU WILL DO IT**

_____

**SIGNATURE**

From *Small Group Strategies* by Laurie Polich and Charley Scandlyn. Permission to reproduce this page granted only for use in buyer's own youth group.This page can be downloaded from www.youthspecialties.com/store/downloads   password: smallgroup
Copyright © 2005 by Youth Specialties

## LEVEL 6: CHALLENGING STUDENTS TO LEAD OTHERS IN SERVICE.

27. Mission Scavenger Hunt—Have your students create a scavenger hunt with a purpose! Any listed items that students collect will be donated to missions. So things like canned goods, clothes, and blankets are all fair game. Have your students find out what is needed first, then make up the scavenger hunt and invite their friends to join in. This is great way for kids to lead other kids into service—and have fun doing it!

28. Create and Lead a Service Project—Get your small group to plan a service project for your youth group. Give them a list of resources— such as Habitat for Humanity, World Vision's 30-Hour Famine, a local soup kitchen, or an assisted living facility—and let your students plan the entire thing, including publicity, transportation, food, follow-up, and so on.

29. Student-Led Mission Trip—Students who have gone on mission trips for a couple of years are ready to lead their own! Equip them with resources to do a weekend or weeklong mission trip—anything from doing a trip with Center for Student Missions (see more information about this organization under Level 1), partnering with a mission's organization at your church, or planning a work week in a location where people need help. Help your students with the contacts and let them plan the whole trip. Be sure to give a report on your trip during or after a church service—adults are extremely encouraged by students who serve.

30. Student Leadership Service Team—Whether you have a leadership team in your youth ministry or not, you can have students form a service team to plan ongoing service projects for your group. They can serve anywhere from six months to a year, and their goal is to plan one act of service per month. Whether it's collecting money to send to a Compassion Child, having a work day at the church, doing the 30-hour famine for World Vision, or passing out lunches on a Saturday after-

noon, your students should be in charge of making announcements, signing up other students, and taking charge of the activity or event.

31. Community Leadership—Review the various places where your students hang out or belong to and—as a group—decide how they could provide a service for that community. For instance, if it is a neighborhood where there are a lot of children, they could organize a kickball game. If one of them regularly visits a grandparent in a convalescent home, the rest of the group could join that person during the next visit and serve for a night by meeting at their group member's convalescent community.

32. Host a Mission Fair—Have your small group partner with your mission elder or pastor and host a mission fair for your church or youth group. Identify local mission projects you can promote. Include domestic and international missionaries, organizations, and projects that you can also invite your church to support through prayer and donations. Divide up all the potential mission candidates among your group and have the students do research to get more information about each of them, such as their philosophy, program, and volunteer opportunities. Schedule a room during weekend services and set up tables to display the information from the various organizations and projects. Ask the local organizations to provide volunteer representatives to be available to answer questions and direct potential volunteers.

# CHAPTER EIGHT
# OUTREACH

HOW BEAUTIFUL ARE THE FEET OF
THOSE WHO BRING GOOD NEWS!
—ROMANS 10:15

The goal for outreach is to create a supportive environment where students are able to bring non-Christian students to hear the gospel message. We also want to equip our kids with the ability to share their faith naturally—in all ways, at all times. Our desire is to foster a passion to share Christ with their friends.

In Romans 10:14-15, Paul reminds us of our calling to the world as Christ-followers:

> How, then, can they call on the one they have not believed in? And how can they believe in the one of whom they have not heard? And how can they hear without someone preaching to them? And how can they preach unless they are sent? As it is written, "How beautiful are the feet of those who bring good news."

Outreach is not a program, it is a reflection and outpouring of our lives. Here are some ideas for outreach at each level of your small group.

## LEVEL 1: HELPING STUDENTS DISCOVER THAT THEY HAVE SOMETHING TO SHARE.

1. The Case for Christ—One of the ways students discover they have something to share is when they learn more about the validity of their faith. The student edition of *The Case for Christ*, by Lee Strobel, is an excellent resource to go through as a small group. There are nine chapters in the book (enough for a two-month study), and each contains important information regarding the person of Christ. Reading this book will empower students with evidence that Jesus truly was the Son of God.

2. The Case for the Resurrection—Divide your group into three teams. Tell them they are a group of lawyers, and they have to come up with an argument to disprove one of the alternative theories to the resurrec-

tion of Christ—"body stolen" (Jesus' body was stolen by the disciples), "wrong tomb" (everyone went to the wrong tomb), or "Jesus didn't really die" (he only fainted and then revived). Afterward, have them talk about their arguments as a group, decide which theory is most convincing, and consider whether these theories cause them to be more or less convinced of the reality of the resurrection.

3. Man on the Street Interviews—This idea is designed to help your students discover the kinds of questions people are asking today and their varying perspectives on the issues that affect our world. Students need to be more aware of other people's viewpoints so they can also be prepared to respond to them whenever they have the opportunity to do so. Hopefully, your students will see that God actually speaks to the questions that are on people's minds.

Assign students to interview people about the topic you're discussing. For example, have them interview a dating couple, a married couple, and a divorced couple on the topic of healthy relationships. They could also interview their friends at school about what stresses out high school kids the most. Or they could ask people a question like, "What would you like to ask God?" At your next small group meeting, discuss the answers people gave. Examine God's response to each of the areas addressed in the interviews.

4. From the Bible to Life—Either before the meeting or by doing some brainstorming with your students, make a list of truths about God's nature, Jesus' teachings, and some biblical principles. Ask your students to choose something from the list and come up with a contemporary song, movie plot, or television drama that illustrates or contradicts that truth. This will help your students discover how God's Word speaks to their culture. It also gives them a way to make the truths of the Bible more understandable and relevant to their friends.

5. From Life to the Bible—Have one of your students share a personal story or childhood memory. Challenge the rest of the group to think of any biblical themes or stories that surfaced during the student's story—as many as they can. Allow them to be as random as possible. Then work together to think of a way this story could be used as a ministry opportunity. For example: "I stole something and felt really guilty about it until I finally confessed." The story of Zacchaeus (Luke 19) could be referenced, as well as Romans 3:23,24 ("For all have sinned and fall short of the glory of God, and are justified freely by his grace"). This story could be told as a way to help friends open up and reveal their own guilt or sin, at which point the student could then share how to experience God's forgiveness.

6. Pictures of Jesus—This idea is meant to help your students expand their mental images of Jesus, connecting his timeless truths to their real-world experiences. Choose a story from the Gospels and have students describe—or even draw—pictures of the scene. Let their imaginations run wild with details of the surroundings, the people, and other images. Have them bring in their other senses, such as smell and sound. After you've heard (or seen) their descriptions, ask what the scene would look like if it happened today. In what way(s) could the truths of the story speak to today's world?

## LEVEL 2: HELPING STUDENTS FIND OPPORTUNITIES TO CONNECT WITH NON-CHRISTIAN FRIENDS.

7. Movie Review—Take students to review a movie (either in the theaters or on video). Have them look at the values, teachings, and claims the movie makes and consider what it seems to be saying to teenagers. Challenge them to push some of the movie's ideas and themes to their logical conclusion. In other words, ask questions like, What would freedom without accountability really look like? Is love at first sight really possible? When you love someone, does that give you license

to pursue that person, no matter the cost? Where does love without justice (or justice without love) lead? This helps students think critically about their culture and learn to engage in thoughtful discussions with their friends and families.

8. Deconstructing the Simpsons—Have your students watch an episode of *The Simpsons*. Ask them to find, examine, and unpack any teaching moments in the episode and the message each one conveys. (One professor found nine major theological teaching moments in one Thanksgiving episode.) Have them think of a way they each could use *The Simpsons* (or some other popular TV show) to open the door to share their faith with a friend.

9. Culture Assessment—Bring in a teen magazine or a videotape of a TV show that is relevant to your students. Work together to deconstruct the ad campaigns it contains. Examine which messages and ads line up with Jesus' teachings and which ones don't. For the ones that don't, ask what Jesus would teach about those behaviors instead. Talk about how these ads can be a springboard to sharing their faith with their friends.

10. Everyday Hero Awards—To make a connection with people outside of your group, create an award to give to classmates, friends, or family members when your students observe them doing a kind, thoughtful, or courageous act. Students could give out the award on their own, or bring the recipient to your next group meeting and present it during a little ceremony. The idea is to connect within your students' circles of influence by saying, "We know you're doing good things." Noticing the good in someone else is the best way to make a connection.

11. Environmental Exercise—Today's postmodern teenager is very environmentally conscious. Why not have your small group sponsor a save-the-earth day, a clean-the-park afternoon, or some other environmentally friendly exercise so your group could invite their

friends to pitch in? Allow conversations about spiritual matters to flow naturally during these events rather than scheduling a special speaker to share the gospel. One group we know of that tried this activity had a student pray at the end and another one had someone read a scripture passage—but these were both student driven.

12. Response Team—Create an ongoing ministry team that responds to school projects, community needs, and neighborhood concerns with volunteer support. Friends and acquaintances can join, too. This team can help with school productions, community events, disaster relief, and support during a crisis. The idea is for students to have opportunities to make a difference in times of need. If one of these already exists on your campus, invite your students to join.

## LEVEL 3: COMMITTING TO PRAY AND CARE FOR FRIENDS AND FAMILY OF STUDENTS IN THE GROUP.

13. Prayer Journals—This idea helps your students realize that prayer is an integral part of outreach. Invite your students each to be proactive about praying for the needs of others by keeping a "prayer journal," in which they record the names of the people they are praying for and how and when they pray for them. Have them choose three to five people (keep the number manageable) that they will pray for consistently. Once a month, bring the names in your students' journals to the whole group for prayer. Keep a record of how God is working in those people's lives and periodically ask the students to share updates about them throughout the year.

14. School Prayer—Take your group to pray for the high school(s) where the students in your group attend. Take a prayer tour of the school—stopping to pray in the lunch area, the football field, the gym, and the corridors. Pray for students at the school, the teachers, parents, the learning that happens there, safety, community across race and

grade barriers, and spiritual openness on the campus. Close by praying specifically for the student(s) in your group who attend that school.

15. Crisis Team—Help your small group become a first-response team. Whenever a crisis affects the lives of a group member's friends or family—your group responds! One small group we know of was the first to learn about someone who was in a car accident that left some of the passengers hospitalized. They organized prayer support, hospital visits, homework help, and baby-sitting for that family. This experience motivated them to be available to respond to any crisis that might come their way.

16. Family Prayer Challenge—This idea will help your students reach out to the most important people in the other small group members' lives—their families! Choose prayer partners, but instead of praying for each other, each partner commits to pray for the other person's family. Make sure each student is aware of his or her partner's needs so as to share accurately and intelligently. You could even have people bring in family photographs to give to their partners as reminders to pray. Writing the requests on the back of the card or photos is another way to help your group remember to pray.

17. Listening Journals or "Covert Praying"—This idea is meant to help students shift their focus off themselves as they become more sensitive to the needs of others. Ask your students to start listening to people with a "spiritual ear." Rather than looking for ways to respond while the other person is talking, challenge them to become more sensitive to a person's needs just by listening to them. Encourage them to record in their listening journals whatever prayer needs they've perceived in the lives of those they've been in conversation with throughout the week—friends, family, and acquaintances. They should also keep up-to-date with the people they are praying for during follow-up conversations—without letting the people know they've been praying for them.

## LEVEL 4: CREATING SPECIAL SMALL GROUP ACTIVITIES FOR STUDENTS TO INVITE FRIENDS.

18. Lady and the Tramp Night—This is a fun activity for a guys' small group to do with a girls' small group. And because it involves both sexes, it has great outreach appeal. The guys make up invitations for a *formal* dinner, instructing the girls to dress up for the occasion. In the meantime, unbeknownst to the girls, the guys dress way down (shabby jeans, T-shirts, no shave). When the girls arrive, they sit at one end of the table (where silverware has been provided). The guys sit at the other end of the table (with no silverware). Spaghetti is served—and the fun begins. After a messy dinner, they retire to another room where *Lady and the Tramp* is shown.

19. Group Creative Date—Have your small group plan a creative date night. One idea: Set up two or three formal tables at McDonald's or some other fast-food restaurant. Tablecloths, silverware, china—the works! Order Big Macs and have them eat their food with a fork and a knife. Another idea is to have everyone meet at one student's house for pizza and a great guy/girl movie (like *How to Lose a Guy in 10 Days* or *Never Been Kissed*). Afterward, you can have a discussion about how realistic the movie was concerning dating relationships. Have your small group brainstorm some creative date ideas they can use to reach out to their friends.

20. Friends Night—Encourage your small group to invite three to five friends (preferably friends they've been praying for) to a "Friends Night." Make popcorn and cookies to eat during the "Friends Marathon"— where they watch their favorite episodes of *Friends*. (For an alternative, you could also rent movies with friendship themes.) Use it as an opportunity to reach out to your students' friends and to give these friends an opportunity to meet the members of your small group. Follow up the evening by inviting them to attend your youth group anytime.

21. The Passion—*The Passion of the Christ* was a huge movie and had a huge impact. As a small group, you can use this movie as an outreach tool by inviting friends to a "Passion Q & A Night." Choose to host this event in the home of a student whose family owns a large- screen TV and have everyone in your small group each invite three friends to come. Before the event, pray together that God would speak to those friends through the movie. Afterward, have a Q & A time where students can dialogue about any question they may have about the film. Many people who were unfamiliar with the Bible saw this film, and it's a great way to connect the emotional impact of the film with the truth of the gospel.

22. Special Guests—Invite a Christian teacher, coach, or another familiar adult from your community to talk to your group during a breakfast, lunchtime, or evening small group that is open to friends. The guest would address a topic that relates to his or her specialty but is also helpful to students. A coach could talk about pressure and athletic performance, a teacher could address some issues that students will face in college—but they would speak to those issues from a Christian perspective. The idea is to provide a forum for students to hear a Christian viewpoint about important and relevant subjects.

23. Hosting Q & A—This idea is meant to provide a forum where students can practice discussing difficult and controversial cultural issues with their friends which will ultimately help them to intelligently engage with these issues in the future. Invite an expert in a chosen field (with a Christian perspective) to answer questions about a controversial topic. Make sure the meeting environment is non-threatening yet open for serious questioning and disagreement. Have students write out questions beforehand so the presenter can prepare. One small group we know of brought in a Christ-following anesthesiologist who used to perform abortions before he came to faith, and they invited their friends to dialogue with him about his firsthand experience with

the abortion issue. Make sure your students follow up with their friends afterward and continue the dialogue.

## LEVEL 5: HELPING STUDENTS LEARN HOW TO SHARE THE GOSPEL.

24. The Spirituality of Outreach—This idea is meant to help your students understand that we don't manufacture genuine outreach; it is a result of God's Spirit leading us. Do a series that links the spiritual disciplines to outreach. The series might look something like this—

*Prayer and Outreach:* How prayer makes us better listeners and more sensitive to God's leading. Exercise: Have students each pray for opportunities to share their lives and faith with someone every day for the next seven days. Have them pray for those people God has put on their hearts.

*Worship and Outreach:* How worship makes us more dependent on what God does rather than on what we do. Exercise: Discuss the fears associated with reaching out to others. Next, have each student take a 10-minute walk with God. During the walk, invite each student to experience the vastness of God and his sovereignty and to give their fears of outreach over to him. Regroup and process each person's experience.

*Discipleship and Outreach:* How our *lives* are a better testimony of God's love than our words. Exercise: Write the fruits of the spirit on index cards (one per card) and tape them to a wall or window where everyone can see. One at a time, have students stand up in front of the group, select one of the fruits of the spirit, and describe (in a minute or less) how that particular characteristic could impact the people they are reaching out to.

The idea behind each of these exercises and topics is to teach students to be dependent on the spirit of God when it comes to outreach. It is also meant to challenge your students to discover how using these spiritual disciplines in their day-to-day lives can impact the people around them.

25. A Case for Faith—A great resource for helping students confront and understand some of the questions surrounding the Christian faith is the student edition of *A Case for Faith* by Lee Strobel. You can use it for a book study with your students or challenge them to study the book on their own and bring their questions to small group. From the topics covered in the book, create exercises to teach students how to articulate their answers to some of the tough questions about the faith.

26. Three Story Evangelism—This method of evangelism (Your Story—Their Story—God's Story) originated at DC/LA, a Youth for Christ event. Students learn that revealing their own stories and listening to others stories are necessary prerequisites to telling *God's* story.

To do this in your small group, challenge your kids to write down "their story"—personal testimonies of their life (how and why each came to know Jesus). Then challenge them to take the time to listen to a friends tell their stories in the coming week—in other words, they should try to find out something more about their friends' lives by taking the time to really listen to them. Then encourage your students to find the connecting point—how they can share their own story of faith with their friends. The last step (which can only take place after a relationship has been formed) involves looking for opportunities to share God's story. This "three story evangelism" encourages kids to build relationships with people *before* they share their faith. And it helps students realize that they can share their faith simply by sharing their lives.

27. What Can We Learn Series—Do a series where you invite students of different faiths (Muslim, Hindu, Jewish) to speak to your small group. (Make sure your guests know this is not a grill session.) The idea is to provide a forum for discovery and appreciation. Develop questions beforehand that the speakers can use for preparation. This type of presentation will help create a nonthreatening environment between people of different religious backgrounds, and it will provide your students with some helpful information as they learn about the unique contributions of other faiths. It will also help clarify the distinguishing features of their own faith.

28. Letters from a Skeptic—The goal of this idea is to help your students engage intelligently with the more sophisticated questions of the faith. *Letters from a Skeptic,* by Gregory A. Boyd and Edward K. Boyd, shares a clear and concise running dialogue that took place over three year's time via the exchange of more than 30 letters between an intellectually skeptical father and his Christian professor son. Read a letter from the dad (the skeptic) to your students and then discuss how they would answer that particular question before you read the answer from the son (the Christian). Ask them if they or any of their friends have had the same question. Then read the answer and discuss if they think it is adequate.

## LEVEL 6: HELPING STUDENTS DEVELOP OUTREACH OPPORTUNITIES FOR THEIR CIRCLE OF INFLUENCE.

29. Ministry of Reconciliation—Have your students identify areas of disunity, hostility, and unresolved conflict on their school campus and start working to begin a ministry of reconciliation.

Step One: Pray for reconciliation.

Step Two: Invite others to be a part of the reconciliation process.

Step Three: Meet with the leadership of the groups who are at odds and introduce the idea of a reconciliation meeting.

Step Four: Hold a meeting with all interested parties to create a plan for how to proceed.

Step Five: Follow up with all involved and present an agreed-upon plan for peace.

This idea could range from something as small as a broken friendship to something as dangerous as warring gangs. Some in-between examples of the need for reconciliation are people from different races, faiths, and economic backgrounds. One white student we know of began praying with Christian African-American students for racial reconciliation on their campus.

30. Ministry Team—Call on each student in your group to lead their own ministry team. Spend an evening brainstorming all the various ministry team possibilities—tutoring, clean-up, missions, school hospitality, and so on. As the leader, they would be responsible for their ministry team's development, culture, management, leadership, and growth. The two-fold purpose of the team would be 1) to help their school or community, and 2) to create a ministry they could invite their friends to join.

31. Intentional Community—Have students in your small group commit to partner with Christians of another race at their school, meeting with them on a regular basis to talk about some of the barriers that exist between them. Have them commit to meet regularly (lunchtime, after school, one evening a week) for a set period of time, during which they can openly and honestly discuss the struggles created by racial diversity. Invite other students to hear the dialogue. Share with them about how God enters into the equation. Use the community ideas in

chapter 4 to create opportunities for them to build relationships outside of the regular meetings. The goal is to establish on their school campus a racially reconciled community—driven by the love of Jesus Christ.

32. Confession Booth—On a college campus during a huge annual party, a small group of Christians opened up a confession booth. People thought they were supposed to come in to confess, and instead it was the Christians who did the confessing! They talked about how the church had wronged people (i.e., the Crusades) and how Christians had failed to be the church Jesus intended us to be by exercising judgment without compassion, not caring for the poor, etc.. The students dressed as monks and welcomed anyone who would listen. But instead of forgiving others, they asked people to forgive *them!* It was a great lead-in to significant discussions about perceptions people had about Christians and the church. Give this idea to your students and let them be creative about how to do something like this on their campus, in their community, or even during a school function.

33. Join a Cause—Dozens of organizations have resulted from significant social issues—many of which carry Christian values and principles. Some examples are SADD (Students Against Drunk Driving), AA (Alcoholics Anonymous), NA (Narcotics Anonymous), Alanon (Families of Alcoholics), and so on. Challenge your students to get involved in one or more of these groups or to form their own groups if a significant social issue arises in their community. This can be a bridge between meeting significant needs and introducing others to Christian principles and values.

34. Bag Lunch and the Bible—One student we know of decided he would do outreach on his campus by starting a lunchtime Bible study. It started with three people and eventually grew to 15! Students brought their lunches and were free to ask any questions they had about Christianity. Adult guests (youth pastor, volunteers) were invited to sit

in on the group—but it was entirely student led. It was a great way for that student to gather with other Christians on his campus and provide a non-threatening forum for those students who had never been to church.

# CHAPTER NINE
# STORIES OF
# SMALL GROUPS

## JOHN

John led a group of freshmen guys. They were unchurched skaters from pretty decent family backgrounds. One obvious strength of the group was that these guys were all really good friends. John was going nowhere in his weekly small group meetings, so he decided he would capitalize on the group's strongest trait: their relationships. He went for a Level 3 community bonding experience and had a sleepover at the church. (Keep in mind that enduring an overnighter with freshmen guys is like undergoing medieval torture while listening to elevator muzak.)

That night the guys were as wild as any freshmen guys have ever been. They never went to sleep; instead, they ended up running downtown in their boxers at 4 a.m. From the outside, this experience looked like a total disaster. But John looks back on that night as the turning point for his group. From that point on, his group began to grow in all levels of spiritual development. Four years later, these guys are key leaders in ministry—they've continued in their own spiritual growth and are now small group leaders themselves.

## JEANETTE

Jeanette had a group of sophomores: cliquey, stuck-up, cute church girls who would only talk about this one guy they all had dated. Jeanette decided that these girls needed a challenge. She confronted their superficiality and went for a Level 6 community strategy. The girls all knew the concept of the open chair, where everyone is supposed to be willing to invite someone new into the group, but they never seriously considered it.

Then one day Jeanette mentioned that she had someone to fill the chair. Her name was Christina, a girl who was incredibly brilliant, deeply mature spiritually, and physically handicapped. She was also looking for some friends. After approaching her group with the idea, Jeanette set things in motion. It was blessed from day one! Chris' very presence helped the small group members move past their shallow self-centeredness. Her insights were a refreshing contribution to the meetings. Deep friendships blossomed. And six years after graduation, Chris and these girls are lifelong friends.

## LAURIE

Laurie's group of juniors got more than they bargained for when Crystal, one of their group members, got pregnant. Immediately, the group was thrust into Level 4 service as they sought to meet the needs of this girl.

After much counsel, Crystal decided to give the baby up for adoption—so one of the group members had her mom research adoptive families. As Crystal's stomach grew, the girls in her group kept her from feeling alienated by standing by her side and sitting with her in church. At the end of the pregnancy, since the father was out of the picture, Crystal needed help delivering the baby. Two members of her small group became her Lamaze partners—and they ran to be by her side when the baby was born.

## LOOKING BACK

When we see our small groups as ministries, rather than just meetings, God opens opportunities for growth and development in ways we could never imagine. Sometimes we are present for defining moments in our students' lives. But most of the time, it's only when we look back that we can get a glimpse of all that God has done in the lives of our students.

## CHARLEY

Charley was a youth pastor who took over a small group of freshmen guys in a fractured and hurting ministry. To be honest, he wasn't very good at running a small group. He had a lot of other things on his plate. He was sometimes unprepared and often a little overwhelmed. But he hung in there with these guys for four years, and he watched God take them to new levels in their small group.

Four years after high school, these guys began graduating from college. One of them, Will, moved back home and became a small group leader with the church. That alone would have made all the years of ministry worth it. But three months after moving home, Will was involved in a tragic climbing accident. While climbing with his younger brother, Will fell 40 feet and hit his head on a rock, just below his helmet. The fall put Will into a coma.

The guys from Will's small group were devastated but quick to respond. They flew in from around the country to gather in Will's hospital room, and they held hands in a circle around his bed—just like they had done a hundred times as a small group. They took turns praying, weeping, thanking God for Will, and saying good-bye. Will died shortly after that.

Will's small group wasn't about a meeting; it was about a ministry—a ministry of hundreds of little steps that God used to take them to supernatural places. And that day Charley got to see a glimpse of all God had done.

God invites you on this journey of helping your kids get to the next level—and then the next and the next. And one day you'll look back and it will all be clear. That's small group ministry!

# BIBLIOGRAPHY

Arrington, D.B. *Home is Where the Art is:An Art Therapy Approach to Family Therapy.* Springfield, IL.: Charles C Thomas, 2001.

Jones, Tony. *Postmodern Youth Ministry.* Grand Rapids, Mich.: Youth Specialities / Zondervan, 2001.

Marcum, Walt. *Living in the Light: Leading Youth to a Deeper Spirituality.* Nashville, Tenn.: Abingdon, 1994.

Miller, Don. *Blue Like Jazz: Nonreligious Thoughts on Christian Spirituality.* Nashville, Tenn.: Thomas Nelson, 2003.

Myers, Joseph R. *The Search to Belong: Rethinking Intimacy, Community, and Small Groups.* Grand Rapids, Mich.: emergentYS/ Zondervan, 2003.

Ortberg, John. *The Life You've Always Wanted.* Grand Rapids, Mich.: Zondervan, 1997.

Willard, Dallas. *The Spirit of the Disciplines: Understanding How God Changes Lives.* New York: HarperCollins, 1991.

RETAIL $9.99

What is a small-group exactly?
What do I do?
What don't I do?

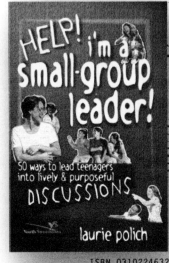

ISBN 0310224632

Twenty-year youth worker veteran Laurie
Polich answers tough questions and explains
50 methods and approaches to small-group
ministry—like building community, accountability, and trust. It's straight to the point, solid
advice for anyone looking to lead a small
group, not just run one.

www.youthspecialties.com/store

Youth Specialties

RETAIL $9.99

**"Questions change people,"** writes
Laurie Polich. Jesus frequently used
questions to inspire, to challenge,
and to demonstrate his love.

ISBN 0310240239

You have an opportunity to do the same:
Inspire. Build community. Use Laurie's
600 well-crafted questions about spiritual
life, the Bible, and more to go deeper in
conversation with your students. It's an
essential resource for youth workers and
volunteers.

www.youthspecialties.com/store

**Youth Specialties**

Ever wish youth group fun and games could accomplish more than burning off students' high-octane energy?

RETAIL $16.99
ISBN 0310255325

It can—if you have the right tools at your disposal. And your number-one tool is Experiential Youth Ministry Handbook.

This innovative resource provides intentional activities with a purpose, specific program sequences, and adaptable templates for making games resonate with your students' minds and hearts.

www.youthspecialties.com/store

Youth Specialties